THE POLITICAL ECONOMY
OF ISRAEL

THE POLITICAL ECONOMY
OF ISRAEL

Ira Sharkansky

Transaction Books
New Brunswick (U.S.A.) and Oxford (U.K.)

Library of Congress Catalog Number: 86-25090
ISBN: 0-88738-117-0
Printed in the United States of America

Library of Congress Cataloging in Publication Data

Sharkansky, Ira.
  The political economy of Israel.

  Includes index.
  1. Israel—Economic policy.   I. Title.
HC415.25.S49   1987   338.95694′054
ISBN 0-88738-117-0

Contents

List of Figures and Tables

For Dr. Erich Horn

Preface

This book began when I read that Israel's government expenditures exceed the country's gross national product. For me, that single fact speaks volumes: about the unusual dependence of Israeli public finance on income from overseas, the great weight of the Israeli government in the economy and society, and the clumsiness of a government whose formal reach is beyond its capacity to act wisely. Add to the size of the Israeli government the political elements of intense political competition, the failure of any party to win a majority in a national election, and coalition governments, and the result is clumsiness in governing the economy.

Chapter 3 documents and explains how the total of governmental and quasi-governmental expenditures have exceeded Israeli GNP. Other chapters illustrate the implications of this centerpiece: for the behaviors of Israeli policymakers; for the problems they encounter when they try to untangle and rearrange the lines of policy that have accumulated over the years; and for the problems of analyzing Israel when the overwhelming dominance of its government sets the country apart from conventional standards of comparison.

The analysis of a complex and dynamic polity carries its own risks. If this book has succeeded its capturing the underlying currents of Israel's political economy, its principle findings will remain useful even as details change. Between the original drafting of the manuscript and its final preparation for the press, the rate of inflation decreased markedly. The annual rate was 400 percent for 1984, but extrapolated out to an annual rate of only 14 percent for the period of October 1985 through April 1986. As detailed in chapter 7, however, Israel's experience with high inflation may not be entirely a matter of history.

Numerous scholars and Israeli officials helped in developing the various analyses included in this book. The dedication is for Dr. Erich Horn. His diligent critiques reflect a wisdom polished by having observed policymaking from the inside and the outside from the 1930's onward. He also is father-in-law, friend, and social conscience.

IRA SHARKANSKY

1

The Political Economy of Israel

The resurgence of political economy as an important topic reflects the deep interpenetration of politics and economics. There are few economic issues of consequence that are not shaped by governmental decisions, and there are few governments whose agendas are not dominated by economic issues.[1]

No country may reflect the mixture of politics and economics as much as Israel. From 1976 to 1981 official reports of spending by governmental and quasi-governmental bodies ranged from 97 to 105 percent of gross national product! How a government can spend so much of its nation's resources is only one of the fascinating questions in Israel's political economy.

Israel also stands out for the critical nature of its economic issues, and the challenges faced by politicians and civil servants who would guide or control the economy. Perhaps any government that spends over 100 percent of GNP is as much a problem as a source of solution. There is also inflation, a negative balance of payments, growing foreign debt, and a stagnation in economic growth. Israeli prices moved upward at an annual rate in excess of 100 percent during 1980-85, and increased at about 1,000 percent on an annual basis during various months in 1984 and 1985. The balance of payments is chronically negative; it averaged 22 percent of GNP in each year during the 1973-84 period. The nation's foreign debt increased from 23 percent of GNP in 1959 to 125 percent of GNP in 1984. Although GNP per capita grew by an average 9 percent per year in the 1959-73 period, it grew by only 15 percent during the entire 1973-84 period (i.e. 1.3 percent per year).

The Theme

Israel's political economy reflects the confluence of several phenomena:

- During the first two and one-half decades of Israel's independence—from 1948 to 1973—there was an impressive record of economic growth despite multiple adversities.

1

- Times have changed. There is no longer—and no immediate prospect of—the large-scale immigration that contributed to rapid economic growth in the past.
- The central role of the government in economic activities facilitated growth in the past. Now the government may be as much of a problem as a benefit. Although Israel's politicians have shown impressive measures of will and success in making war and peace, they have recently lacked both will and success in economic policy. The country's recent history as reviewed by its economists offers a depressing picture of misallocated resources, and a failure to make or persist with decisions that have unpleasant implications.[2] Perhaps heroic or messianic decisions are out of place in modern political economies that are finely tuned amidst conflicting interests.[3] Issues of inflation, employment, foreign exchange, living standards, and the government budget are linked together in tangles of causes and effect. A drastic change in one of these variables can have unpredicted and unpleasant implications for others.
- There remains vitality among Israeli politicians, and among the career professionals who do much of the work involved in proposing and implementing public policies. Despite the heavy weight of formal procedures that are centralized in government ministries, it is befitting the inhabitants of the Jewish state that they behave as entrepreneurs within their public sector, sometimes ignoring or evading the laws that they have enacted against themselves. Also, they are willing to pursue policy goals indirectly when circumstances deter a direct pursuit of their goals. Officials break the formal rules frequently. Sometimes they break the informal rules as well. It can be difficult sorting out the violations that are permitted in the interest of flexibility, and the violations that are condemned as corruption. The disorder in Israeli politics that has contributed to some of its problems may also reflect the vitality that will be its salvation.

Environments That Shape and Constrain

To understand the how and why of economic policy in Israel, it is necessary to comprehend key features of the country's history, its economy, and policy goals that are widely accepted. The following points describe the environment within which Israelis make their economic decisions.

- Israel is a country of immigrants and the children of immigrants. The Jewish population[4] swelled from 600,000 to 1,810,000 in the first 10 years of national independence (1948-58), mostly on the strength of survivors of the European Holocaust, and mass movements from North Africa, Yemen, Iraq, and Iran. Despite the hardships associated with the first years in a new country, the population growth and economic integration of the immigrants—together with the economic and human

capital that they brought with them—created the wherewithal for substantial economic growth that persisted with short periods of setback
until 1973. (The events of that year included a devastating war, and the
beginning of an international inflation that affected Israel no less than
other countries.) Moreover, the filling of a new country permitted economic policy-making to go forward without concern for entrenched and
conservative agrarian or aristocratic elements that retarded moderniza-
tion in other developing countries.[5]

- Israel's defense posture dominates the scene. There have been five or six
  major wars in less than four decades of independence, and numerous
  additional confrontations with terrorists both inside and outside Israel.[6]
  The country's continuous military footing costs its economy upward of
  20 percent of GNP annually.[7] The prominence of defense contributes to
  the dominant role of the state in economic affairs. The widespread
  service in the defense forces, and the consensus that assigns high priority
  to defense supports a nationalism that is also rooted in older periods of
  Jewish history. This facilitates large roles for the state and other public
  bodies, and leads Israelis to accept personal sacrifices for the public
  good.[8]

- The hostility of Israel's Arab neighbors has implications that go beyond
  military preparedness and defense outlays. Israel is denied free access to
  regional markets. Elsewhere its ability to compete is affected by higher
  shipping costs, and hostilities related to Arab boycott efforts. Also because of boycott efforts, Israel is not viewed as a convenient place for
  investment by international firms.

- Like other developing countries, Israel has depended on foreign sources
  of capital to finance growth, and a strong government to manage capital
  recruitment and investment. Earlier waves of capital were brought by
  immigrants, contributed by overseas Jews, or paid by the West German
  government as compensation to victims of the Holocaust. More recently, there have been major loans and grants from the United States
  government, and loans from banks arranged by the Israeli government
  or by Israeli commercial banks and business firms.[9] In recent years,
  Israel's balance of payments has been affected by the need to pay escalating sums to its creditors. Moreover, Israeli economists write that much
  of the country's investments have been misallocated; that Israel's capital
  plant and equipment is underutilized; and that government programs
  and procedures that were suitable for an earlier day may be barriers in
  the way of the progress that is demanded now.[10]

- The government is not the only public body with a dominant role in the
  economy. During the period of the British Mandate (1919-48) the Jewish Agency and the Labour Federation (Histadrut) provided social services, employee representation, and employment opportunities. Both
  organizations retain important roles. The Labour Federation, in particular, must be counted among the giants of the Israeli economy. Its

bank, pension funds, insurance companies, and construction and manufacturing conglomerates account for some 25 percent of the country's employment and a substantial part of its investment capital. Given the fact that the Labour Federation is both employer and employees' representative, it lends a peculiar cast to the form of neocorporatist economic policy-making that occurs in Israel.[11]

- No major economic policy can go forward without the cooperation of the Labour Federation. The highly politicized policy-making structure of the Labour Federation (with national elections, a parliament, and executive and judicial bodies parallel to those of the state) means that major policies generate public controversy and substantial politicking in the Labour Federation as well as in the state sector.[12] Although Israel qualifies as a genuine democracy by virtue of free elections, a lively media, and extensive public debate, the weight of large institutions that claim to speak for sectors of the public means that—as in other neocorporatist settings—[13] individuals can be frustrated in expressing their own preferences.[14]

- Israel pursues several policy goals that enjoy wide consensus among its political leaders. These reflect key features of the present environment and national history, and serve both to guide and to constrain policymakers. The tenuous nature of Israel's existence, and the dominant Zionist ideology put a premium on attracting and retaining a sizable Jewish population. Emigration is to be avoided, as are economic problems—like unemployment or the erosion of private savings—that are likely to produce emigration. Economic policymakers have been constrained from draconian steps against inflation that would produce a step-level increase in unemployment. The government has been pressured into the continued funding of inefficient industries that employ unskilled people in peripheral "development towns." Also, the government has committed substantial resources to guarantee the stock issues of commercial banks that—before their collapse—had become vehicles for mass savings.

- High inflation during 1977-85 was partly a manifestation of these policy constraints. The linkage of wages, savings, rents, and other payments to the cost-of-living index meant that inflation was perpetuated by the mechanisms that are designed to protect the population from its worst effects. The lack of intense public pressure to do something about high inflation is traceable to these linkages. Incomes and savings moved upward along with inflation. Although the public was protected from the loss of livelihood or savings as a consequence of inflation, managers in business and government had to struggle with decisions that are made difficult by constantly changing prices and a lack of predictability. The low growth that has marked Israel's economy in recent years may owe something to the problems of financial planning and control that are traceable to inflation.[15]

Israel's extreme and unique characteristics lend themselves to phrase makers. It can be said that it was the most successful of the developing countries. Per capita income grew at over 5 percent annually between 1950 and 1970,[16] all the while that the country absorbed masses of immigrants made wretched by their previous experiences, fought several wars, and created a democratic polity that has proved to be stable.

The predominance of the government in Israel's economy makes it the most socialist country outside the Eastern Bloc. Along with a government budget that exceeds gross national product, there are numerous detailed controls on the activities of government officials, private-sector companies, and individual citizens.

Israel is bound with countless governmental controls, and it also is a noisy democracy with a bit of anarchy. Few groups seem willing to accept what is due to them routinely, according to the formal rules. It is Israel's fate to suffer the worst from the centrally controlled East and the demo-cratic West. Informally agreed evasions of the formal rules are part of Israeli life. Perhaps the economy cannot function without flexible admin-istration that permits circumventing the "snarls of central planning."[17] Among the problems of officials and citizens is knowing the boundaries of the informal rules, and what they can expect by way of exposure and punishment if they seek too much from informal arrangements.

The economy has moved, perhaps prematurely, to a deemphasis of in-dustry and the growth of services, on the model of European and North American economies.[18] Thus, it has made a rapid transit from *developing country* to *post industrial* or *de industrial country* without stopping to enjoy a period of mature stability. Israel's high inflation, debt, and foreign dependence, along with its economic, social, and political successes lead pundits to wonder if its future will be like Scandinavia, or Latin America.[19]

The country is both Spartan and Athenian. The enormous military sector has penetrated virtually every civilian institution via the appoint-ments of retired officers.[20] Yet, the very extent of the military sector may keep Israel from becoming a military state! With such a large portion of the citizenry in the military, there are military personnel at all points of the political compass. "Pacifist generals" have retired to important roles in the government as representatives of the Labour party, and even further to the left in antiestablishment parties that have sought accommodations with Palestinian groups that are conventionally described as "terrorist."

The Athenian side of Israel appears in orchestras, museums, and univer-sities that rank well on international scales of comparison. The high level of education is thought to be an asset in economic competition. At least one economist, however, worries that the country has invested too much of its assets in education.[21]

The distinctiveness of Israel makes it both fascinating and troublesome. The country presents a laboratory for comparative study. Its unusual traits highlight in sharp relief certain problems of politics and economics (like the intertwined issues of large government, active democracy, aggressive demands for services, and high inflation) that also exist elsewhere, but in lesser dimensions. Yet, Israel may be so unique that it cannot be compared usefully with other countries. Perhaps it is interesting only to those who are fascinated by it, or as a case that illustrates the known outer limits of certain political or economic features.

Framework for Analysis

This general discussion of Israel's economic and political traits provides the setting for chapters that explore strategic points of the country's political economy. Chapter 2 documents a number of distinctive features of Israel's government, economy, and politics, and explains how they complicate the use of standard concepts for analyzing the country. Chapter 3 offers several indicators for the size of the Israeli government, ranging to financial outlays that exceed the gross national product. Chapter 4 explores the issue of Israeli standards of living; among other things, it follows on the lessons of chapters 2 and 3, and shows how conventional indicators of personal well-being can be awry in an economy that is so heavily socialized. Chapters 5 and 6 deal with various aspects of *who gets what?* in Israel: chapter 5 assesses the capacity of local government officials to exhibit *fiscal prowess* despite the formal structure that emphasizes the dominance of central government ministries; chapter 6 looks at the distribution of resources in the government budget during a 7-year period of high inflation. Chapter 7 shows how Israel's high inflation is linked with a complex system of alleged causes and effects, which frustrates analysis and treatment.

Chapters 8-11 pursue qualitative analyses of Israeli problems and the strategies for dealing with them. Chapter 8 finds that a number of Israel's prominent problems are *conundrums* (i.e. problems without solutions). This means that appropriate strategies involve *coping* rather than *solutions*.

Chapters 9-11 detail three kinds of behaviors that serve Israeli policymakers as coping mechanisms. Each has its advantages and disadvantages. It is a matter of some dispute as to whether—in the final analysis—each lessens or aggravates Israel's problems. Chapter 9 describes *entrepreneurial* behavior that occurs at important places in Israel's public sector. Chapter 10 describes the *indirection* that appears in Israeli policy activity when officials encounter constraints that keep them from pursuing their goals directly. Chapter 11 examines the informality and flexibility that prevail in Israeli government. Flexibility provides some of the underpinning for entrepreneurialism and indirection. It also invites inquiries into the troublesome boundaries between flexibility that is acceptable, and corruption that requires punishment. Entrepreneurialism, indirection, and flexibility with respect to the formal rules facilitate policy-making in the presence of severe constraints. At the same time these behaviors are among the factors that complicate orderly problem solving.

Chapter 12 takes an overview of Israeli politics, to remind the reader of important other issues that compete with economics for the attention of the country and its policymakers. Finally, an epilog asks if there are clear prescriptions to be made for Israel's political economy.

Notes

1. See, for example, J.E.S. Hayward and R.N. Berki, eds., *State and Society in Contemporary Europe* (Oxford: Martin Robertson, 1979).
2. Yoram Ben Porath, "The Economy of Israel: Maturing Through Crises" (Jerusalem: Falk Institute, 1985).
3. R.N. Berki and Jack Hayward, "The State of European Society," in *State and Society in Contemporary Europe*, ed. J.E.S. Hayward and R. N. Berki (Oxford: Martin Robertson, 1979), pp. 253-64.
4. Which amounted to 82 percent of the population at the end of 1948 and 83 percent at the end of 1982 (in both cases the reference is to the population of Israel defined by its officially declared boundaries).
5. Moshe Syrquin, "Economic Growth and Structural Change in Israel: An International Perspective" (Jerusalem: Falk Institute, 1984).
6. The 1948 War of Independence; the Sinai Campaign of 1956; the 6-day War of 1967; the 1970 War of Attrition (sometimes not counted as a separate war); the Yom Kippur War of 1973; and the War in Lebanon of 1982-85.
7. Eitan Berglas, "Defense and the Economy" (Jerusalem: Falk Institute, 1983).
8. Russell A. Stone, *Social Change in Israel: Attitudes and Events, 1967-79* (New York: Praeger, 1982).
9. Ruth Klinov, "Israel's Changing Industrial Structure: Years of Growth and Years of Slowdown" (Jerusalem: Falk Institute, 1984).
10. Joram Mayshar, "Investment Patterns in Israel" (Jerusalem: Falk Institute, 1984).
11. Philippe C. Schmitter and Gerhard Lehmbruch, *Trends Towards Corporatist Intermediation*, (Beverly Hills, Calif.: Sage Publications, 1979).
12. Haim Barkei, "Theory and Praxis of the Histadrut Industrial Sector" *Jerusalem Quarterly* 26 (Winter 1982): 96-108.
13. See Berki and Hayward, "The State of European Society"; Frederick B. Pike and Thomas Stritch, eds., *The New Corporatism: Social-Political Structures in the Iberian World*, (Notre Dame: University of Notre Dame Press, 1974).
14. Michael Shalev, "Labor, State and Crisis: An Israeli Case Study," *Industrial Relations* 23 (Fall 1984): 362-86.
15. Michael Bruno and Stanley Fischer, "The Inflationary Process in Israel: Shocks and Accommodation" (Jerusalem: Falk Institute, 1984).
16. Syrquin, "Economic Growth and Structural Change in Israel."

17. James C. Scott, *Comparative Political Corruption* (Englewood Cliffs, N.J.: Prentice-Hall, 1972), p. x.
18. Ben-Porath, "The Economy of Israel."
19. Syrquin, "Economic Growth and Structural Change in Israel."
20. Alex Mintz, "An Empirical Study of Military-Industrial Linkages in Israel," *Armed Forces and Society* (forthcoming).
20. Klinov, "Israel's Changing Industrial Structure."

2

Israel Is Like Other Countries, But Different

Each of the world's 160-plus independent countries has some claim to being unique. Most of these claims can be accepted as true but can be relegated to secondary importance in the quest for general patterns. France is European as well as being French. The United States joins France in the category of well-to-do Western democracies, as well as having numerous traits that are distinctively American. Both of these countries, and many others find their places in established categories on the conventional indicators of governmental structure, political behavior, and economic and social traits. Distinctive traits add subtlety and instructive exceptions to the comparative picture.[1] Distinctive national traits also justify those political scientists who elevate contextual and experiential analysis to higher intellectual standing than wholesale comparison using macroeconomic and macropolitical indicators.[2] In most cases, however, distinctive traits do not hinder comparison.

The concepts of *distinctive* or *unique* do not lend themselves to precise measurement. It is probably the case that all countries have some traits that put them in categories with other countries, and have other traits that defy the search for something similar elsewhere.

Israel is like other countries in some traits. It has earned a place in lists of countries that are democracies; are pluralistic; have mixed economies; and have bureaucracies that are rational and competent. More than other countries, however, Israel seems to exhibit a number of traits that are distinctive, if not actually unique. These traits are more than oddities. They have significance for Israeli policymakers, who are inclined to use standard measurements and classifications in their analyses; policymakers of other countries who are charged with monitoring Israeli activity; and social scientists concerned with Israeli phenomena. Individuals must tread carefully if they would draw lessons from Israeli experience for application elsewhere, or make recommendations to Israelis on the basis of what has occurred in other countries.

The Distinctive Traits of Israel

This description of Israel's distinctive traits is guided by the importance of various elements with respect to Israel's politics and public policy. Most prominent are the size and dominance of Israel's government. Also important are several additional features of Israel's economy and politics that are distinctive on the world scene, and join with the character of the government in leaving their mark on policy issues, and on the ways that individuals and institutions deal with these issues.

Israel's Distinctive Government and Other Public Sectors

Israel's government and its quasi-governmental extensions seem to be the largest in all the democratic polities. Chapter 3 explains how the finances of these bodies have exceeded 100 percent of the nation's GNP in recent years. Israel has built the most socialist country outside of the Eastern Bloc.

One element in the government's dominance of the economy—and distinctive in itself—is Israel's military. The defense budget regularly takes between 20 and 30 percent of GNP, and has approached 40 percent in periods of war and resupply. The typical parallel indicator in other Western countries has ranged between 1 and 5 percent of GNP in the 1970s and 1980s. Also, the official reports of Israeli defense spending *underestimate* its real size. They do not take into consideration the substantial "opportunity costs" represented by military service. Males spend a significant amount of their productive years in uniform: 3 years from the age of 18, and then between one and three months per year in the active reserves until their midfifties. Many females spend two years on active duty from the age of 18, and some do reserve duty for a few years after that.[3]

Israel is also distinctive in the extensive public bodies that exist outside the government. The country has three public sectors: that of the government; that of the Labour Federation (Histadrut); and that of organizations that straddle the boundaries between Israel and the international Jewish community.[4]

Israel's Labour Federation does more than represent workers in negotiations with management. It is also management for much of the economy. The Labour Federation operates industrial, construction, financial, commercial, and social service organizations. Its employees amount to some 25 percent of the country's work force, and its Sick Fund provides most Israelis' medical care. Its banks, pension funds, and insurance companies account for a substantial amount of the country's capital. The great extent of membership in the Labour Federation (members and their families amount to 58 percent of the population) means that elections for the Labour Federation offices attract the participation of the major political parties, and figure in the country's "political business cycle." There was a wave of governmental generosity, and a reluctance to take harsh economic measures both prior to the national election of July 1984 and the Labour Federation election of May 1985. The multiple roles of labor representative, employer, banker, and international trader make the Labour Federation a major factor second only to the government itself in economic policy-making.[5]

Perhaps the most obviously unique feature of Israel is its being the only country in the world with a Jewish majority. This deserves comment in connection with several issues of politics and public policy. Here, it is important in filling out the description of Israel's public sectors. One of the public sectors straddles the blurred boundary between Israel and overseas Jewish communities. Numerous organizations are built on the model of an international board of directors and cadre of professional employees, voluntary fund-raising in Jewish communities throughout the world, and projects undertaken in Israel and abroad. The most prominent is the Jewish Agency, which is responsible to the World Zionist Organization. The World Zionist Organization includes elected representatives from more than 60 national Jewish communities. The Jewish Agency traces its history to the period of the British Mandate (1919-48) when it was a social service body with a politically selected directorate, and the authoritative voice for the Jewish residents of Palestine with respect to the British administration. The Jewish Agency retains extensive responsibilities for immigration to Israel; development in the fields of agriculture, housing, and industry; and the provision of social services.

The Jerusalem Foundation illustrates numerous Israeli bodies—independent of the Jewish Agency and World Zionist Organization—that collect funds overseas. The Jerusalem Foundation is also distinctive governmentally. It is a private foundation created and led by Teddy Kollek, who has been mayor of Jerusalem for the past 20 years. The foundation has the standard board of distinguished directors, but Kollek is the acknowledged dominant force. He uses the foundation to pay for projects in Jerusalem that the municipal council cannot or will not finance. He also uses the foundation to leverage matching funds from the municipal council, national government ministries, and nongovernmental sources. The foundation's income and disbursements approximated 16 percent of the municipality's operating budget in 1980. Its projects are widely appreciated for their significant additions to the city's beauty and its cultural and social programs, and it is looked at with skepticism by those who worry about the mixture of public and private roles. The conventional mechanisms of political accountability do not reckon with elected officials who use independent resources for public activities.[6]

Israel's Distinctive Economy

One point has already been made about the distinctive character of Israel's economy: the large role played by the government. This is reflected not only in the size of the government budget in relation to GNP but also in the role of the government in setting wages and prices. The Finance Ministry is important in defining personal incomes not only because some 25 percent of the work force is on the government's payroll but because of the leverage that the ministry exercises in private- sector wage negotiations via the government's subsidies to industries and social agencies, and national agreements on the indexation of wages to the consumer price index.

By means of the subsidies provided to consumer goods and services, the Finance Ministry—along with other ministries—sets prices for basic foods, public transportation, and health and educational services. There are also standard prices for automobiles and other major purchases. During periods of major economic crisis, the government extends its price controls to many additional consumer goods and industrial inputs.

The government also asserts itself in regard to economic details via the indexing of bonds, insurance policies, mortgages, rents, pensions, taxes, court judgments, and other transactions—as well as wages—to the consumer price index. Israel's indexing is extensive by international standards.[7]

Indexing affects several issues of public policy, especially during a period of high inflation. It minimizes public demands for strong action against inflation,[8] and limits the options of a government that wants to fight inflation. The government could cut its budget significantly by reducing subsidies, and thereby lessen one stream of public spending that contributes to inflation. However, reductions in subsidies serve to increase consumer prices, and through indexation boost wages and other costs, both for the government and other bodies throughout the economy. Moreover, the linkage of wages and many savings schemes keep the public's resources moving upward, and complicate the government's efforts to curtail consumer spending.

The Israeli economy is also dependent on what happens outside the country to an unusual extent. The country's ratio of imports to GNP was .7 in 1978, while the comparable ratio was .15 for a group of developed countries and .21 for a group of developing countries.[9] The balance of payments is a constant source of worry; the exchange rate between the Israeli shekel and foreign currencies is often in the spotlight of policy disputes; and subsidies for exports are a major item in the budget. Israeli economic specialties like diamond polishing, tourism, and military exports are vulnerable to prosperity, recession, or international conflict overseas.

Israel's agricultural exports vary with the weather in Israel itself, as well as in the countries whose products compete with Israel's in Western Europe. When Spain and Portugal entered the European Common Market in 1985, Israel's agricultural planners anticipated a reduction in their own sales due to the favored terms granted to members of the Common Market.

During the first 25 years of independence, from 1948 to 1973, Israel's economy was one of the distinctive international successes, even while the country absorbed mass immigration and fought several wars. Its GNP per capita grew by more than 8 percent per year during 1959-73, for example, after controlling for inflation.

Israel's economy ceased being a source of pride with the Yom Kippur war of 1973, and subsequent increases in the price of petroleum. During 1977-84 annual growth in GNP per capita dropped to an average of less than 2 percent. GNP per capita actually declined, after controlling for inflation, from 1981 through 1984. Now Israel may have the highest foreign debt per capita in the world, and its inflation rate has competed with those of Argentina and Bolivia for first place.

Israel's Distinctive Politics

Israel's politics reveals several distinctive features that derive from the Jewish characteristics of the society. One of these is the Zionism that serves as national ideology.[10] There is also the need for the government to cope with anti-Zionism or anti-Semitism that is officially inspired or widespread in Arab and other countries. Anti-Israel postures appear in different countries as official declarations of war, a lack of formal recognition or the exchange of ambassadors, economic boycotts, and anti-Israel actions in the United Nations and other international bodies. Among Western governments, Greece, Ireland, and the Vatican have so far refused to exchange ambassadors with Israel.

Also derived from Jewish history is the worry of numerous Israelis that they may once again fall to a military conqueror who will not be content with territorial demands but will carry out policies of mass destruction and dispersion. Political leaders and commentators cite catastrophes from 3,500 years ago to the recent past.[11] The list of miserable experiences features Egyptians, Babylonians, Greeks, Romans, plus a series of unpredictable European and Arab rulers. The Nazi Holocaust competes for prominence on this list with Arab terrorist attacks against schoolchildren and other civilian targets. From such fears derive the obsession of many Israelis with a strong military, and their ambivalence toward foreign powers who offer assistance. The special relationship with the United States is said to be vulnerable to the same kind of Great Power considerations that led the once-supportive Great Britain and France, each in their turn, to declare arms embargos when Israel's enemies mobilized along its borders.

Zionist ideology and the fragility of the Jewish state also explain the sensitive role of emigration in policy considerations. Emigrants threaten the Zionists' goal of gathering to the Jewish homeland the exiles of 2,000 years. Emigration also threatens a lessening of physical security in the midst of hostile neighbors that already have many times the population of Israel. Some politicians have labeled emigrants "traitors." At the same time, there are programs of government aid for groups vulnerable to emigration—like young people released from compulsory military service—and for overseas Israelis who want to return home. The fear of emigration figures prominently in economic policy-making. During the period of high inflation, governments have avoided reductions in government expenditures that are likely to bring about an increase in unemployment. Ministers cite the experience of recession in the mid-1960s, when a spurt of unemployment to 10 percent was associated with substantial emigration. From 1977 through 1984, unemployment was as low as 2.9 percent on an annual basis, and did not go above 5.5 percent.

Conflict between religious and secular Jews is another prominent feature of Israel's politics. Israel officially proclaims itself a Jewish state, but religion and rabbis cause turmoil. In most of Israel's history, religious parties have held a critical number of seats in the government coalition. They have used their weight to advance their interests, or hold off the further secularization of the society.

Contentious issues between religious and secular Jews include the regulation of marriage and divorce; abortions, autopsies, and other medical practices; the excavations of archeologists and building contractors that may disturb ancient Jewish graves; behaviors that are prohibited on the Sabbath and religious holidays; the availability of pork and other foods that are prohibited by religious doctrine; the obligations of religious Jews to serve in the military; plus government funding for religious schools and other institutions.

Religious-nationalist zealots identify with maximalists in Jewish history, and set themselves against state authorities who are not considered sufficiently concerned with Jewish interests. They urge expanded settlement in the territories occupied during the Six-Day War, and a harder line against Arab terrorists. Groups that are variously labeled the Jewish underground or Jewish terrorists (depending on one's position toward them) have been responsible for acts of violence against Arab individuals and property.

Perennial conflicts between coalition partners is itself a distinctive feature of Israeli politics. No party has won a majority in any of Israel's eleven national elections. The coalition nature of governments is among the factors said to limit the policy options that could be effective against high inflation and increasing national debt. For each proposal of a retrench-ment-minded finance minister to cut the budget, there are likely to be counterproposals from ministers attached to other parties or factions of the finance minister's own party.

The dominant role of the government in the economy has its own im-plications for Israeli politics. The well-being of each economic sector is likely to depend on one or another kind of governmental decision: favora-ble terms of credit; government purchase of company shares; the prices that can be charged for products or services; the exchange rate that is applied to the goods that a firm purchases from overseas; the taxes applied to the firm's products or services; welfare payments; salaries; the degree to which wages and other items are linked to the cost-of-living index. In late May and early June 1985, for example, the following political-economic events commanded the attention of the mass media and the government:

- The 1,400 employees of Ata—an old and inefficient textile firm—de-manded that the government save their company from bankruptcy. Workers demonstrated at the Knesset and the home of the prime minis-ter; laid themselves down on the main highway outside one of the plants; occupied the plant for several consecutive days and nights; and tried a hunger strike. Some workers screamed about their frustration at having dedicated their lives to the firm and now finding themselves at an ad-vanced age with no other source of support for their large families; others cried in front of the television cameras.
- A television documentary reported that Zim—the national shipping line—was in even more dire straits than Ata, the textile company. Zim was affected by a general decline in the fortunes of international ship-ping, had debts that were some 20 times those of Ata, and was locked into high salary scales that made it noncompetitive with foreign firms.
- Workers at the Timna copper mine—which traces its ancestry to the time of King Solomon but is not competitive in the contemporary mar-ket—threatened to ignite dynamite in the company offices if the govern-ment went ahead with a plan to close the company.
- Schoolteachers cancelled selected days or hours of instruction, and threatened to interrupt the national high school baccalaureate examina-tions because they could not reach agreement with the government about payment of a wage settlement; the government asserted that the present economic crisis required budget cuts and layoffs, even of tenured teachers.
- Postal workers, taxi drivers, hospital personnel, and court clerks also struck, or declared work limitations, as part of their demands for higher wages or service fees, and the employment of more personnel to help with the work load, or protests against government budget cuts.

- Dispute continued about proposals of the Finance Ministry to charge a monthly fee to the parents of schoolchildren, and to increase the tuition at universities.
- Work was continuing on the water channel from the Mediterranean to the Dead Sea, despite what seemed to have been a government decision to suspend work on the project, and to provide only enough money for "closing down" expenses.
- An official delegation of U.S. economists visited with key ministers and bureaucrats. Their mission was to oversee Israeli government commitments to implement economic reforms in exchange for $1.5 billion in emergency aid, which was in addition to approximately $3 billion in other aid from the United States government.
- The Paris air show included an exhibit of the new Israeli fighter plane, indicating that work was going forward on the multibillion-dollar project, despite continuing assertions that it was not justified on the grounds of cost, military advantage, or guarantee of independence in weapons acquisition.

At the same time, the country's agenda also featured a number of contentious issues dealing with security, religion, and nationalism. Together with the economic issues, they illustrated the frenzy amidst multiple intense problems that characterize Israeli politics.

- One emotional storm centered on the exchange of more than a thousand convicted Arab and other terrorists for 3 Israeli soldiers held prisoner by one of the Palestinian organizations that had fought in Lebanon. For many Israelis, the price paid was too high, especially insofar as two of the soldiers had shown inadequate resistence before their capture, and were censured by the military command. The media were filled with protests from the parents of schoolchildren and the relatives of other victims killed by the terrorists being released from prison.
- A second storm centered on religious Jews convicted or on trial for participating in acts of violence against Arab targets. Their supporters attacked the release of Arab terrorists while the Jews remained in jail.
- A third storm centered on a proposal to set up a commission of inquiry into the origins and conduct of the war in Lebanon. Opposition political parties proposed the commission, partly to threaten the government coalition between Labour and Likud. Some members of the Labour party—which had been in the opposition during most of the war—supported the inquiry, but the Likud bloc threatened to bring down the government if the inquiry went forward.
- The country noted the third anniversary of the war in Lebanon, and the 18th anniversary of the Six-Day War. Israeli troops patrolled in a "security strip" in the extreme South of Lebanon, and supported the unof-

ficial "Army of South Lebanon." It was hoped that this army would provide security throughout that region—and help protect Israel's northern border after the Israeli army completed its withdrawal from Lebanon.

- A government commission made its report on the murder of a leading figure in the Labour party. The murder occurred in 1933 (sic), was said to be politically inspired (although it was never solved officially), and had caused occasional eruptions of accusation and counteraccusation between the major parties.
- A television documentary covered the exposure and execution of an Israeli spy in Damascus during 1965. Persons interviewed as part of the documentary asserted that Israel's intelligence service had not taken appropriate measures to protect its agent.
- King Hussein of Jordan generated two issues with a visit to Washington: one that seemed likely to set the Reagan administration against the Israeli government and its supporters in Congress over the sale of sophisticated weapons to Jordan; the other over the details of a U.S.-Jordanian-Palestinian-Israeli initiative to advance the cause of peace in the Middle East.

Implications for Policymakers and Political Science

Several of Israel's distinctive features get in the way of those who would judge the country according to international norms. These problems fall equally on Israelis and foreigners, policymakers and political scientists.

One problem concerns the concept of gross national product. This is widely used as a standard for judging the government's use of available economic resources. However, the standard is more bizarre than instructive because various measures of government finance exceed GNP.

A related problem is the use of personal or family income to assess Israeli standards of living. The government's huge budget includes money to provide free—or highly subsidized—services that citizens of other countries must buy on the open market. Chapter 4 will indicate that Israeli living standards, as a result, are higher on the international scale than suggested by money incomes alone.

Several policy options that are feasible elsewhere come up against the distinctive nature of Israel's international setting, or the distinctive features of its economics and politics. Cutting military expenditures is a popular option for other democracies intent on reducing inflation. However, this option clashes with the continued intransigence of Israel's enemies, and the wide support that the military enjoys in the Israeli population. The military budget offers the largest target for a finance ministry that is inclined to cut, and the military budget did decline in real terms after the withdrawal from the Sinai under the Camp David accords. Yet military expenditures were still 21 percent of GNP in 1982, and increased to 23 percent of GNP in 1983.

Any severe cuts in the government budget are to be avoided if they are likely to increase unemployment, and the emigration that is thought to be triggered by unemployment.

The extensive indexation of the Israeli economy limits other conventional ways of dealing with inflation. Government budget cuts for subsidies of food and public transportation, for example, increase the cost-of-living index and thereby increase wage payments to employees throughout the public and private sectors.

The unusual dependence of the economy on foreign trade also constrains economic policy-making. Devaluations of the shekel help Israeli export industries in world markets but add to the cost-of-living index—and boost inflation—via increased prices for imported consumer goods and industrial inputs. For much of the period of high inflation, it has been simpler to keep the shekel overvalued, and to subsidize export industries. These subsidies also add to inflation. They represent part of the no-win feature of an economy that seems locked into inflation by the multiple roles of the government in the economy.

Even that most conventional of analytical tools—describing a country as a cultural and political manifestation of its region—encounters problems in the Israeli case. Other countries of the Middle East do not welcome Israel in their region, and many Israelis think of themselves as something other than Middle Eastern. Yet, the physical presence of Israel in the Middle East is unavoidable, as well as being the cause of security and economic problems.

The Israeli society is a mixture of Middle Eastern and European roots; however, even these categories are misleading. "Middle Eastern" Israelis originated in a number of Asian and African countries ranging from Afghanistan to Morocco, plus Greece, Turkey, Georgia, Soviet Central Asia, and Bulgaria. "Europeans" hail from Eastern and Western Europe, North and South America, Australia and New Zealand. Moreover, most of the Middle Easterners and Europeans were marginal figures in their former societies. It is more accurate to describe the Israeli culture as Jewish, affected by a variety of national origins; however, this single-case category offers limited help in comparative analyses.

More than other countries, Israel is a country without peers. It is alone, or at least distinct from the conventional norms on a number of dimensions that are used by policymakers and political scientists. It is fascinating in its own right, as demonstrated by the prominence it occupies in the mass media of countries that are friendly or antagonistic.

The Advantages of Examining a Distinctive Country

There are reasons for looking closely at Israel in order to understand political-economic workings under extreme conditions. Israel reveals in sharp detail several phenomena that may shed light on events elsewhere, or serve to warn policymakers elsewhere what may occur if they travel too far down the road taken by their Israeli colleagues:

- Israel's extensive indexation shows how multiple linkages to the cost-of-living index can moderate the social costs attendant on high inflation. It also shows how extensive indexation complicates the task of any government intent on reducing inflation that has gone beyond modest proportions.
- Israel's combination of a heterogeneous society and proportional representation illustrates the capacity of proportional representation to assure diverse perspectives in the national parliament. It also illustrates the problems associated with such diversity: Israel has never enjoyed a government composed only by one political party, with the political strength to define or implement policies that threaten disadvantages to one or another social group.
- Israel demonstrates a government that prioritizes its goals in the presence of intense demands. Issues of national defense have taken priority over issues of economic policy. Defense has received more attention by the government, and the government has been more willing to make difficult decisions and expend vital resources in the case of defense. The government carried on a war in Lebanon for more than three years, at a human cost of more than 650 deaths, despite the claims of opponents that the war was unnecessary. Israel's initial attack and persistence in pursuing military objectives are described by their supporters as preventive actions, designed to destroy the military infrastructure of groups that planned and executed acts of terror against Israeli targets. In the same years the government dithered over several approaches to deal with its economic problems. In the absence of a clear economic policy, inflation increased over the 1977-84 period from 35 percent to almost 400 percent annually, and foreign debt increased from 104 percent to 125 percent of GNP.
- Israel's intense pressures in both military and civilian sectors, and the tightness of a highly centralized formal structure of government provoke a variety of informal mechanisms for making policy. Chapters 9-11 describe the phenomena of public-sector entrepreneurialism, policymaking by indirection, and a pervasive willingness to break the formal rules. These coping mechanisms do not solve Israel's problems. Informal gaming by one policy-maker seems to provoke countergaming by policymakers with contrary interests. Israel is a lively arena for observing government, but with much frustration for its policymakers.

The fascination with Israel may reflect the fact that its experiences are not unique, even while their character is distinctive. In a number of fields Israel presents extreme manifestations of issues that have occurred elsewhere. Its military accomplishments have been impressive against numerous adversaries. Its political accomplishments include the development of a working democracy (with extensive criticism of officeholders and the peaceful transfer of power) amidst difficult conditions. Its stable democracy has caught on in a population that came mostly from the lower strata of European, Asian, and North African autocracies. Israel's bureaucracy has developed along rational models, with opportunities for political favoritism but little bribery. Its economy developed rapidly, integrated immigrants from several score countries, and produced a distribution of resources that is egalitarian by international standards.

A continuing challenge of Israel's economy and polity is to deal with inflation and foreign debt that have been Latin American in their proportions, and with continuing foreign and domestic disputes while maintaining established patterns of democracy and egalitarianism.

The problems of comparing Israel systematically with other countries recall the expressions that Israel is a country built by a people who lived without a country for 2,000 years; and that Jews are like other people, only different.

Notes

1. Mattei Dogan and Dominique Pelassy, *How To Compare Nations: Strategies in Comparative Politics* (Chatham, N.J.: Chatham House, 1984).
2. Charles W. Anderson, "System and Strategy in Comparative Policy Analysis: A Plea for Contextual and Experiential Knowledge" in *Perspectives on Public Policy-Making*, ed. William B. Gwyn and George C. Edwards III (New Orleans: Tulane University Press, 1975), pp. 219-41.
3. Eitan Berglas "Defense and the Economy: The Israeli Experience" (Jerusalem: Falk Institute, 1983).
4. See the author's *Wither the State? Public Enterprise in Three Countries* (Chatham, N.J.: Chatham House, 1979), ch. 3.
5. Michael Shalev, "Labour, State and Crisis: An Israeli Case Study," *Industrial Relations* 23 (Fall 1984): 362-86.
6. See my *What Makes Israel Tick? How Domestic Policymakers Cope with Constraints* (Chicago: Nelson-Hall, 1985), ch. 6.
7. Gustav Donald Jud, *Inflation and the Use of Indexing in Developing Countries* (New York: Praeger, 1978).
8. Michael Bruno and Stanley Fischer, "The Inflationary Process in Israel: Shocks and Accommodation" (Jerusalem: Falk Institute, 1984), p 35.
9. Nadav Halevi, "The Structure and Development of Israel's Balance of Payments" (Jerusalem: Falk Institute, 1983).
10. The central theme in this many-faceted ideology may be expressed as support for the Jewish homeland in Israel (i.e. Zion). See Shlomo Avineri, *The Making*

of Modern Zionism: The Intellectual Origins of the Jewish State (London: Weidenfeld & Nicolson, 1981).

11. Yehoshofat Harkabi, *The Bar Kokhba Syndrome* (Chappaqua, N.Y.: Rossel Books, 1983).

3

Israel's Bizarre Public Finance: Governmental and Quasi-Governmental Bodies That Spend More Than 100 Percent of Gross National Product!

This chapter deals with an issue that has profound importance for many features of Israel's political economy: the large size of the government and other public sector bodies. The finding that governmental and quasi-governmental bodies spend *more than 100 percent of gross national product* reflects the enormous power that resides in official hands. There are few economic issues that do not depend on decisions of officials. From their economic power flows influence over the most intimate details of personal lives: incomes, prices, savings, investments, housing, education, health care, and recreation. Wherever Israelis turn, they find one or another governmental body with a role in what they are planning for themselves.

The large size of the government budget also reflects extensive and cumbersome controls within the government sector. Departments, municipal authorities, and companies owned by the government live within a thick network of connections with the Finance Ministry and other bodies that examine what they intend to do, and provide or withhold their permission.

The extensive nature of government also causes problems for those who wish to measure its size. Although this is a problem not only of Israel, it may be particularly severe in Israel due to the large size of government. Numerous bodies claim a degree of independence from government, even while they depend on government financing. Identifying what should be labeled governmental requires a knowledge of the country's organizational landscape.

Israel's government is known as a high spender. The International Monetary Fund showed it in first place among Western democracies in 1980, with expenditures amounting to 76 percent of GDP. Ireland and Sweden were a distant second and third at 51 and 41 percent of GDP.[1] An examination of Israeli sources shows aggregate financial activities of governmental

23

and quasi-governmental bodies substantially above the IMF report. Budget outlays of the government varied between 80 and 85 percent of GNP for fiscal years 1978-82.[2] Israel's Central Bureau of Statistics reported a larger conception of spending by "government, local authorities, and national institutions" that varied between 95 and 105 percent of GNP during fiscal years 1977-81. "National institutions" receive voluntary contributions from abroad, and—in coordination with governmental officials—invest in economic development and support the provision of social services.[3]

This chapter identifies a number of items not included in the government budget or the official compilations of the Central Bureau of Statistics. Because of some overlaps between them and outlays of the government, local authorities, and national institutions, these additional items cannot simply be added to the figures presented above. There is no doubt, however, that the aggregate of governmental and quasi-governmental finances have exceeded 100 percent of GNP for most recent years.

Israel's governmental and quasi-governmental bodies are able to spend *more than the nation's gross national product* because they receive substantial resources that do not figure into the calculation of GNP. There are grants from overseas governments and private contributors, plus loans from overseas and domestic sources.

These bizarre phenomena also reflect the overwhelming dominance of the government in the nation's economy. Israel offers the worst of East and West. Policymakers have economic responsibilities that resemble those of Eastern Europe, in the context of aggressive political parties, labor organizations, and other features of the democratic West.

Israel's variety of democracy seems especially conducive to a large and growing role for government. No party has ever won a majority in elections conducted according to proportional representation. Coalition governments include competitive parties and subparty factions whose leaders seek to bid up the resources available to the ministries they control, or at least to keep a retrenchment-minded finance minister from cutting the budgets of their ministries. The Labour Federation (Histadrut) as well as the government operates mass-employment industries and offers social services. Party competition produced a "political-business-cycle" bidding-up of public goodies both prior to the governmental elections of July 1984 and the Labour Federation elections of May 1985.[4] The inability of the government to ratchet-down from triple-digit inflation during 1980-84 owes something to this difficult combination of a dominant role for government in the economy, and competitive democracy.

Israel's political culture and its hostile international environment also contribute to high public expenditures. Social welfare has been an important value from the time of the Zionist founders. Government investments designed to assure employment opportunities have figured prominently in plans to attract Jewish immigrants, and to dissuade emigration. The well-known defense burden keeps military expenditures in the range of 20-40 percent of GNP annually, compared to the 1-5 percent that is typical of most other Western countries.

Israel's case is extreme, but it has implications for other countries. Even where public expenditures are much smaller percentages of GNP, the aggregate of governmental and quasi-governmental finance is likely to be significantly larger than the figures conventionally reported for government alone.[5] This touches issues as narrow as techniques for governmental accounting, and as broad as the prospects for political accountability in the case of governments whose total activities are not readily apparent. At risk are the conclusions of political scientists and economists that rely on quantitative analyses of financial data made available by governmental and international bodies.[6] Also at risk are the analyses and proposals of policymakers who rely on conventional financial indicators, and the assumptions of citizens that their elected representatives can control government via the budget.

Deciphering Israel's Budget and Other Financial Reports

Finding one's way through Israel's government budget and other financial reports requires a prior knowledge of the country's complex public sectors. Significant finances of several bodies do not appear in the government budget, or in official reports for government, local authorities, and national institutions:

1. Nonprofit health and educational organizations. Important here are the sick funds operated by the Labour Federation and other public bodies that provide full health care to some 90 percent of the population; and the universities. In recent years these bodies have received subsidies from the government for upward of 50 percent of their outlays. At the same time they have had to accept the Finance Ministry's policies with respect to the membership fees and tuition payments that constitute the principal sources of their "independent"income. This independent income does not figure in the financial data reported above. The Finance Ministry has also proved to be an important actor in determining the wage rates and other benefits paid by these organizations, and in deciding about major capital projects and program developments. For these reasons, the sick funds and the universities warrant consideration among the quasi-governmental bodies of Israel. Insofar as allocation of their "independent" income is subject to governmental control, it ought to be included in the reports of public sector finances.

2. Bus transportation. Virtually all of Israel's internal public transportation is provided by two large cooperatives affiliated with the Labour Federation. There is also a small bus company owned by the Beer Sheva municipality. The national government subsidizes these service providers, and has a dominant role in setting the fares that are their major sources of "independent" revenue, and in approving acquisitions of new equipment. As in the case of the sick funds and the universities, the "independent" income of these bus companies also warrants inclusion in public-sector financial records.
3. Directed credits from the Bank of Israel for activities favored by government policy. These credits are administered by the central bank, in cooperation with the commercial banks, but outside the framework of the government budget. Some 98 percent of these credits in 1980 subsidized export activities.
4. Government companies. These represent a sizable extension of the Israeli government. There were 213 government companies, subsidiaries, and joint ventures included in the *Annual Report* of the Authority for Government Companies for 1980, plus an unrecorded number of additional subsidiaries and joint ventures between these organizations and other public and private bodies. The companies recorded in the *Annual Report* employed some 64,000 workers in 1980, as compared with some 86,000 employed in the government ministries. Directors of these companies are appointed by government ministries. Only new government investments in these companies, and the purchase of the companies' goods and services by governmental bodies are included in the government budget figures. The turnover for the companies is the closest approximation available for the overall size of the companies' financial activities. For 1980, this equaled some 35 percent of the government budget.
5. Tax expenditures. These are "expenditures" that the government makes via reductions or forgiveness in certain tax liabilities, when taxpayers use their own resources for stipulated purposes. Israel makes tax concessions for investments in agriculture, industry, construction, tourism, exports, and natural resources; payments to pension funds; and a variety of social services. The latest detailed estimates of tax expenditures were made by the Ministry of Finance for the 1980 budget year, and equaled some 10 percent of the government budget.[7]

Senior personnel in the Bank of Israel and the Central Bureau of Statistics concede the anomalous character of official reports for the finances of government, local authorities, and national institutions that do not also include the "independent" financial activities of nonprofit health and educational organizations. The state comptroller has criticized the Finance Ministry for its failure to include in the government's budget the credit activities of the central bank that subsidize exports.[8] Israel follows conventional practice in keeping most income and expenditure of government companies, as well as tax expenditures, outside the government budget and official reports of governmental finances.[9]

Non-Governmental Public Sector

Israel's complex public sectors include important organizations that have ties with government via close participation in policy-making or joint ventures but that are not so close as the quasi-governmental bodies noted above. Of particular importance are the following:

1. Enterprises associated with the Labour Federation (Histadrut). The Israeli Labour Federation is much more than a workers' organization that bargains for wages and working conditions. It is an umbrella organization that includes industrial, commercial, transportation, and financial bodies; educational, cultural, and sport activities; and the nation's largest providers of medical care and public transportation (which have been counted above as part of the quasi-governmental sector). Some 1,100 firms are owned by the Labour Federation, and another 1,400 cooperative enterprises are associated with it. The families of Labour Federation members include some 58 percent of the nation's population. Some 100,000 workers are employed by firms owned by the Labour Federation, and another 170,000 work in cooperative enterprises associated with the Labour Federation. These two groups of employees amount to some 25 percent of Israel's labor force. The bank of the Labour Federation is Bank Hapoalim (the Workers' Bank). It is the second largest commercial bank in Israel, and—together with its associated pension funds and insurance companies—is a major instrument in the country's institutions for the accumulation and investment of capital. The Labour Federation is governed politically, on the basis of elections conducted in the workplace and in nationwide polls. Israel's political parties compete for seats in the legislative assembly of the Labour Federation, as well as in its executive, judicial, and audit bodies.[10]
2. Bank Leumi (National Bank). This is the largest and oldest of Israel's commercial banks. Like all of Israel's commercial banks, Bank Leumi's activities are closely regulated, and are subsidized by the Bank of Israel and the Finance Ministry. The history and the structure of Bank Leumi makes it even more closely a fixture of the public sector than other banks. It was originally the Anglo-Palestine Bank, established by Theodore Herzl as the banking institution of the Zionist movement to colonize Palestine with Jews. With the coming of the Israeli state in 1948, Bank Leumi served as the government's central bank until the founding of the Bank of Israel in 1954. The World Zionist Organiza-

tion—a body made of up representatives from Jewish communities in some 60 countries—continues as the principal owner of voting shares in Bank Leumi.

Senior personnel in the Bank of Israel, the Finance Ministry, and the Central Bureau of Statistics, and the state comptroller are adamant in asserting that the Labour Federation and Bank Leumi are not governmental. However, they concede that they are not "private" in the conventional nature of that term.

In addition, there are smaller banks responsible to public organizations, which employ political mechanisms for making policy, and which also engage in joint activities with governmental bodies. Notable here are the United Mizrachi Bank, a commercial bank owned and operated by religious Zionists; and several specialized banks responsible to organizations of kibbutzim and moshavim (communal agricultural settlements).

Analysis

How is it possible that Israel's governmental and quasi-governmental bodies spend more than the resources that seem to be available? Some of this amounts to a word game: Israeli governmental and quasi-governmental bodies receive and spend resources that are not, technically, counted as part of the GNP. Partly this is a function of imported resources. Israel's economy is more open than the average. Its ratio of imports to GNP was 0.70 in 1978. In a group of developing countries, the same ratio was 0.21, and in a group of developed countries it was 0.15.[11] In addition, loans and grants from overseas flow to—and are spent by—governmental and quasi-governmental bodies, without their figuring in calculations for gross national product. For 1980, net receipts of international transfers amounted to 16.4 percent of GNP.[12]

Israel's high government spending is also a function of high inflation. Almost 10 percent of government outlays for 1980—when annual inflation was 117 percent—were accounted for by the closed circle between the government and the Bank of Israel of debt repayment and the receipt of additional loans. These transactions—commonly called "printing money"—allowed the government to increase the number of shekels provided to each program. The budget for 1984 (put together when inflation was over 200 percent annually) projected 22 percent of its total outlays for debt repayment to the Bank of Israel alone. Although these transactions appear in the government budget, they do not affect the size of GNP.

Some of the explanation for a government that spends more than GNP lies in Israel's underground economy. There are substantial incentives for tax avoidance where there is a value added tax of 15 percent, and marginal income tax rates of 60 per cent begin at monthly gross incomes that are less than U.S. $1,300. As in other countries, the underground economy adds to national resources without adding to GNP.[13]

Implications for Political Science

Israel's public finances may be extreme manifestations of a government that dominates the economy and conducts much of its public business via bodies that are not, strictly speaking, governmental. However, there are lessons in this case for other countries. In particular, the elusive nature of quasi-governmental activities—and finances—is a problem that appears in numerous countries.

International bodies publish compilations of many countries' financial records, but these bodies have not mastered the variety of arbitrary national accounting practices to produce cross-national data that are comprehensive. As in Israel, the activities of quasi-governmental organizations are especially problematic. The United Nations, for example, indicates that it relies on the various national governments to supply information according to certain formats. Among the caveats noted is one that pertains to the issue of quasi-governmental bodies: "The boundary between ancillary agencies and other government agencies is very difficult to specify precisely, and variations in treatment are likely to lead to incomparability among countries."[14]

Despite problems in gathering the raw data, various analysts have tried to work their way through the tangle to produce some findings and explanations of cross-national government spending. This field of inquiry has been a major enterprise at least since Adolph Wagner laid the foundations some hundred years ago in his widely cited *law of increasing expansion of public activities*.[15]

By going back to a point of Wagner's that has not attracted much attention from his successors, it is possible to find a circularity in the history of government financial activity. He wrote: "Commercial state revenues are historically older and originally predominated; but historical development has caused them, and more particularly the State's own productive revenues, to become much less important in all modern European countries than compulsory activities." Wagner explained the relative decline of state commercial activities by the loss of state lands, the spread of private ownership, and the increased importance of collective activities financed by tax revenues. What Wagner did not foresee—at least in the fragments of his work available in English translation—was a renewed surge of public enterprise activities several decades later. It is part of Wagner's legacy that government statisticians, economists, and political scientists concentrate their effort on the activities of "governmental" bodies, narrowly defined. In the meanwhile the once-archaic "commercial" activities of government have revived and expanded to the point—along with newer varieties of quasi-governmental activities—where they are important enough to render doubtful any studies that ignore them.

Even *The Economist* of London, with its self-styled reputation for being "numerate," can trip in its way through government accounts. In a table labeled "Political Indicators" for 23 countries, it listed Israel's defense expenditures as 31.2 percent of GDP, and total central government expenditures as 33.6 percent of GDP. On the basis of those data it wrote that "Israel stands out with *almost all its central government budget devoted to its armed forces*"(italics added).[16]

The complete parsing of Israeli defense expenditures is an enterprise that goes beyond this book. *The Economist* is far from clear in defining the parameters of its data. From the looks of it, the journal omitted transfer payments and subsidies, as well as debt repayments from what it called "total central government expenditures." This would eliminate extensive social programs, including pensions, welfare payments, and aids to municipalities.

Israel's defense expenditures are more modest than *The Economist* indicates when they are calculated directly from the budget documents without reference to GDP or the concepts associated with it. For budget years 1982-1984 defense expenditures ranged between 17 and 28 percent of the total government budget. Not estimated here is the percentage of debt repayment that should be attributed to the defense sector.[17]

Implications for Policy and Politics

Two kinds of implications for policy and politics flow from this chapter. One pertains to the overwhelming size of the Israeli government, and its dominance of the economy. The government's responsibility for over 100 percent of GNP reflects the multitude of services and controls that originate in government offices. The situation is self-extending, insofar as any industry or social group with a problem looks automatically to government for financial assistance. The inflation that ranged between 117 and nearly 1,000 percent on an annual basis from 1980 to 1985 reflected the centrality of the government in the economy, and the difficulties in refusing claimants. Each of the four men who served as finance minister between 1977 and 1984 identified the reduction of inflation as a major goal; each was frustrated by colleagues in the government who resisted cutting the activities of their ministries.[18] Chapter 7 returns to the issue of Israeli inflation.

A second implication for policy and politics pertains to the complexities in measuring the financial activities of governmental and quasi-governmental bodies. Government statisticians in Israel are hampered by differentials in the timeliness and the quality of financial reports coming from government ministries, local authorities, national institutions, nonprofit organizations, and government companies. Although the government accountant submits financial reports for ministries' activities within six to eight months after the end of a fiscal year, reports from other public bodies may be delayed by as much as three years. Also, some public bodies distort their financial reports so as to seem needy of more government aid, or to seem in compliance with government regulations. The Labour Federation's Sick Fund (which provides medical care to some 76 percent of the Israeli population) is especially jealous of its "privacy" and formal independence of the government. It does not readily open itself to government inspection, despite its dependence on the government for the approval of its fees and for subsidies that make up the great bulk of its revenues. Tax expenditures in Israel—as in other countries—represent a significant use of public resources. However, Israel's tax expenditures have not been estimated since the 1980 budget year. With inflation in the range of 100-1,000 percent annually, delays in financial reporting compound the limitations of those who would make macroeconomic policy.

These aspects of the Israeli case have wider application. Governments generally do not record centrally the financial activities of all their far-flung governmental and quasi-governmental organizations. Policymakers as well as social scientists suffer. Elected representatives can perform only part of the functions assigned to them by democratic theory if they do not know, and cannot vote upon the full range of governmental activities. The sizable accounts that are "off budget," and beyond the range of governmental statistics compromise political accountability and limit those who analyze government finance.

A government's budget may be the principal lever that policymakers use to shape policy.[19] Yet the leverage of government finance over macroeconomic policy is only part of what it might be.[20] It is said that a lever might move the world if there were only a place to anchor it. To use a lever well, however, one must know its size.

Notes

1. *I.M.F. Yearbook 1983* (Washington: International Monetary Fund, 1983).
2. Budget outlays as finally spent, shown as the "gross budget totals" in *Budget Principles*, annually 1980-1984 (Jerusalem: Ministry of Finance, 1980-1984) (Hebrew). The actual percentages from 1978 were 80, 82, 82, 81, 85.

3. *Supplement to the Monthly Bulletin of Statistics* #12, 1982, p. 14; #4, 1984, p. 74; *Monthly Bulletin of Statistics*, July 1979; June 1983; May 1984. The actual percentages frm 1977 were 105, 96, 95, 95, 100.
4. On the general point of Israel's political business cycle, see Yoram Ben-Porath, "The Years of Plenty and the Years of Famine—A Political Business Cycle?" *Kyklos* 28 (1975): 400-3.
5. Allen Schick, *Congress and Money: Budgeting, Spending, and Taxing*, (Washington: Urban Institute, 1980).
6. Patrick D. Larkey, Chandler Stolp, and Mark Winer, "Theorizing about the Growth of Government: A Research Assessment," *Journal of Public Policy* 1, no. 4 (1981): 157-220.
7. Asher Arian and Yoram Haroyah, "Estimates of Tax Expenditures for 1980," (Jerusalem: Finance Ministry, 1981, Mimeographed) (Hebrew)
8. *Annual Report #31* (Jerusalem: State Comptroller, 1983), pp. 89-94 (Hebrew).
9. *Supplement to the Monthly Bulletin of Statistics*, December 1982, pp. 31-32.
10. Gabriel Bertal, *The Histadrut: Structure and Activities* (Tel Aviv: Histadrut, 1982); Histadrut Auditor, *Annual Report #4, 198* (Tel Aviv: Histadrut, 1981) (both in Hebrew).
11. Nadav Halevi, "The Structure and Development of Israel's Balance of Payments" (Jerusalem: Falk Institute, 1983).
12. *Statistical Abstract of Israel 1983* (Jerusalem: Central Bureau of Statistics, 1984), p. 200.
13. Friedrich G. Schneider and Werner W. Pommerehne, "The Decline of Productivity Growth and the Rise of the Shadow Economy in the United States" (Paper delivered at the XIIIth World Congress, International Political Science Association, Paris 1985).
14. *Yearbook of National Accounts Statistics 1981* (New York: United Nations, 1983), p. xii.
15. Richard A. Musgrave and Alan J. Peacock, eds., *Classics in the Theory of Public Finance* (New York: St. Martin's Press, 1967).
16. *The Economist*, December 12, 1983, pp. 55-56.
17. For an analysis that claims that financial outlays do not touch all of Israel's defense costs, see Eitan Berglas, "Defense and the Economy" (Jerusalem: Falk Institute, 1983).
18. Michael Bruno and Stanley Fischer, "The Inflationary Process in Israel: Shocks and Accommodation" (Jerusalem: Falk Institute, 1984).
19. Aaron Wildavsky, *Budgeting: A Comparative Theory of Budgetary Processes* (Boston: Little, Brown, 1975).
20. Murray Weidenbaum, *The Modern Public Sector: New Ways of Doing the Government's Business* (New York: Basic Books, 1969).

4

Israel's Standard of Living

In 1960 Israel's national income per capita stood at 85 percent of the average national income per capita shown by some two dozen Western, developed countries. In 1980 Israel's national income per capita was only 51 percent of the average shown by the same group of Western countries.[1] In the interim, Israel's national income per capita had grown by 180 percent after controlling for inflation. When compared to the greater growth elsewhere in the West, however, Israel's national income per capita had declined by 40 percent!

The relative fall in Israel's national income per capita commands more attention than the increase in the country's national income measured against its own past. The finding challenges the conventional assertion that Israel has been a successful developing country, with one of the worlds highest continuous rates of economic growth, at least until the economic problems of the recent past.[2]

Problems with Income as a Proxy for Living Standards

National income per capita appears to be a useful measure for a country's standard of living. The measure is available over a span of years, and focuses on the economic wherewithal available to the residents of numerous countries. As defined in the United Nations' *Statistical Yearbook*, "National income in market prices is the sum of compensation of residential employees, the excess of property and entrepreneurial income receivable by resident economic agents over the property and entrepreneurial income payable by them and indirect taxes reduced by subsidies."[3]

In Israel's case there are some fundamental problems with the use of national income per capita—or any other income measure—as a simple indicator of living standards. Many of these problems derive from the principal message of chapter 3: the economic dominance of Israel's government and other public bodies. Expressed in simple language, Israel has the most socialist economy of any nation outside of the Eastern Bloc. From this flow several implications.

- The government and other public bodies provide substantial social services at prices to consumers that are below their market cost.
- The government has subsidized basic foodstuffs, public transportation, and fuel.
- Partly because of subsidized commodities and services, and partly because of direct government controls on wages, the overall wage level in the economy is below the Western average for comparable occupations.

Each of these phenomena has the effect of providing Israeli residents with more purchasing power than indicated by the simple measure of monetary income. The questions relevant to living standards are these:

- How much purchasing power do Israelis receive by virtue of the socialist component in their economy?
- How does this affect the country's relative standing on measures of living standards?

Various studies have sought to deal with these issues by comparing the prices paid by Israelis for a standard list of commodities and services whose prices are recorded more or less simultaneously in other countries. A recent study conducted by the European Economic Community found that Israeli prices are generally below those found in the European Common Market. As a result, gross domestic product per capita, personal income, and other standard measures must be adjusted upward from the nominal indicators determined by exchange rates alone.[4]

The problem with these findings is that data are not available on a standardized basis for numerous years over an extended period of time. They provide an indication that Israeli living standards are higher than indicated by monetary income but do not allow an answer to the question of changing purchasing power over the 1960-80 period. If Israeli prices are generally lower than prices in other Western countries but have remained in a similar proportion to them, then the data showing decreasing relative national income per capita from 1960 to 1980 would reflect a decline in living standards.

To deal with the comparison of living standards over time via national income per capita, it is possible to correct the national scores on income per capita by the proportions of national economic resources that are government spending for social services. Where that proportion is high (or low) by international standards, it should add to (or subtract from) the indicator of national income per capita as a measure of living standards.

The formulation that is used here to correct national income is the *proportion of gross domestic product used for nondefense government out-*

lays. To be sure, Chapter 3 has testified to the weakness of GDP as a measure of national economic resources, at least in the Israeli case. However, the Israeli analyst faces a problem: despite the shortcomings inherent in certain conventional measurements, they may be the only ones available for international comparisons. Table 4-1 shows Israel's uncorrected scores for national income per capita over the period 1960-80 compared to a number of Western countries, and parallel indicators that are corrected for the proportion of each country's GDP that is used for nondefense government activities.[5] Because of problems in the availability of reliable data, the corrected indicators are available only from 1970 onward.[6]

Israel's nondefense government expenditures have been higher than those of other Western countries' as a proportion of GDP. Moreover, Israel's nondefense government expenditures grew, as a proportion of its GDP, relative to those of other countries' over the 1970-80 period. As a result, the correction works to *increase* Israeli living standards as measured by national income per capita in relation to the Western average. For most of the indicated years 1970, and beyond, Israel's corrected income per capita figures are higher than the Western average.

Even after these corrections the relative position of Israeli national income per capita declined over the 1970-80 period. The decline is on the order of 19 percent from the 1970 base, instead of the 35 percent shown for national income per capita uncorrected for the nondefense size of government expenditures.

Table 4-1
Changes in Israeli National Income per Capita
(U.S. dollar equivalents)

	1960	1970	1975	1978	1980
Absolute growth (Israel compared to its own past 1960 = 100)	100	188	358	368	502
Absolute growth controlling for inflation in the base of U.S. dollars (1960 = 100)	100	143	197	167	180
Israeli national income per capita as percentage of selected Western countries' average	85	78	69	50	51
Israeli national income per capita as percentage of selected Western countries' average corrected for differences in nondefense government expenditures	n.a.	126	134	93	102

Sources: *United Nations Satistical Yearbook, 1981* (New York: United Nations, 1982), pp. 156f. *Statistical Abstract of the United States, 1982-83* (Washington: Bureau of the Census, 1982), p. 461.
Appendices to Budget Principles, 1980 (Jerusalem: Ministry of Finance, 1980), p. 25.

Other Measures of Living Standards

This discussion of Israel's national income per capita on an international scale only begins the discussion of living standards. The components of living standards, and their weights, vary with the perspectives of different cultures and values.[7] The general concept includes economic resources, plus the quality of life as reflected by such features as health, education, food intake, domestic stability and the absence of crime.[8] Because of complexity in the concept of living standards, and the problems which exist in even the best nation-wide indicators, it is preferable to rely on conclusions built upon trends established over time, and different measurements of living standards.[9]

Economic Wherewithal

The economic component of living standards should not rest upon income per capita alone. The underlying strengths and weaknesses of a nation's economy indicate the wherewithal that can finance individual and public sector activities currently, and define prospects into the future. In Israel's case the examination of several economic components reveals a crucial turning point for the worse at the time of the Yom Kippur War, and other downward turns in several indicators during the most recent two or three years.

The record of Israel's economic development is one of impressive growth until 1973, and serious problems since then. Table 4-2 offers summary indicators, derived from publications of Israel's Central Bureau of Statistics, and corrected for the influences of inflation and population growth.

Israel's gross national product, per capita, grew by an average of 9 percent per year from 1959 through 1973. During 1974-84, the average annual growth in this indicator dropped to 1.4 percent. There was an actual decline of 2 percent in the country's GNP per capita, controlled for inflation, over the 1981-84 period.

One component of Israel's economic resources has been foreign transfers. These include donations from the Jews of the Diaspora, restitutions from the West German government in compensation for the Holocaust, aid from the United States government, and loans obtained by Israeli governmental and nongovernmental bodies. The annual aggregate of these transfers has moved generally downward as a percentage of Israel's current GNP. Transfers averaged 12 percent of Israel's current GNP during 1959-72; they reached a peak of 24 percent of GNP in 1973; and have declined each year during the 1979-84 period.

One source of foreign transfers is loans. These are less desirable than donations and restitutions, insofar as loans must be repaid along with interest. Accumulated foreign debt has increased sharply and consistently as a percentage of Israel's current GNP. The growth over the long 1959-84 period was on the order of 14 percent per year. During 1984 Israel's foreign liabilities had accumulated to the equivalent of 125 percent of its current GNP.

A persistent *negative* balance of payments is a chronic sign of Israel's economic vulnerability. In 1984, however, this indicator was at its least-worrisome level in more than 10 years: the negative balance of payments was *only* 16 percent of the current GNP.

Foreign reserves is an indicator of a country's savings, and its ability to withstand short-term economic reverses. This measure moved upward along with other signs of Israel's economic health during 1959-73, and then dropped precipitously in response to the 1973 war, and the need to rearm. It climbed again through 1982. Its more recent decline has been a prominent subject of worry among the country's economists, and a cause of emergency foreign aid requests during 1984-85.

Israel's unemployment remained below 5 percent of the work force for 20 of the 26 years between 1959 and 1984; however, it has been in the 5 to 5.5 percent range for 3 of the 4 years between 1981 and 1984.

Government spending (including that of local authorities and national institutions) increased more or less consistently from 1969 to the late 1970s. Official reports put the indicator at about 100 percent of GNP. As noted in the previous chapter, however, the aggregate of what is officially reported plus that which escapes the official reports is likely to have exceeded GNP for most recent years.[10]

Israel's defense expenditures are consistently high, and must be taken into account when considering what government programs can contribute to standards of living. Defense expenditures also signify the noneconomic costs imposed on Israelis for living in the Promised Land. They reflect the country's preoccupation with war; the preparation for war; and the prospect of casualties that seem likely—sooner or later—to touch one's family and friends.

Defense expenditures averaged 26 percent of GNP during 1969-83, and reached 38 percent of GNP for the war year of 1973. Furthermore, an Israeli economist has calculated that the official reports of defense spending actually *understate* the totals. For example, the official reports do not include economic opportunity costs incurred by having such a large percentage of the work force in the regular army or on active duty in the reserves.[11] In the other developed, Western countries considered in this chapter, defense expenditures typically ranged between 1 and 5 percent of GNP during the 1970s and 1980s.

Changes in average family income reveal a turning point for the worse in the early 1970s. Family incomes increased by 4.2 percent per year during

Table 4-2

Measures of Israel's Economic Wherewithal, 1959-84

	GNP	Transfer	Foreign Debt	Balance Payments	Reserves	Unemployment	Expenditures	Defense Expend.	Family Income	Inflation
1959	1.00	0.12	0.28	−0.19	n.a.	5.0	n.a.	n.a.	n.a.	2.3
1960	1.07	0.13	0.39	−0.14	0.11	4.6	n.a.	n.a.	n.a.	2.3
1961	1.16	0.08	0.37	−0.15	0.12	4.0	n.a.	n.a.	n.a.	6.7
1962	1.20	0.16	0.60	−0.22	0.25	4.0	n.a.	n.a.	n.a.	9.5
1963	1.30	0.14	0.56	−0.18	0.26	3.6	n.a.	n.a.	n.a.	6.6
1964	1.35	0.11	0.55	−0.20	0.25	3.6	n.a.	n.a.	n.a.	5.2
1965	1.46	0.09	0.53	−0.15	0.24	3.6	n.a.	n.a.	5.51	7.7
1966	1.45	0.08	0.52	−0.12	0.21	7.4	n.a.	n.a.	5.58	8.0
1967	1.43	0.13	0.56	−0.14	0.27	10.4	n.a.	n.a.	5.65	1.6
1968	1.60	0.11	0.61	−0.18	0.25	6.1	n.a.	n.a.	5.90	2.1
1969	1.75	0.10	0.62	−0.20	0.17	4.5	0.63	n.a.	6.24	2.5
1970	1.86	0.12	0.68	−0.24	0.18	3.8	0.67	0.24	6.79	6.1
1971	2.02	0.12	0.72	−0.18	0.24	3.5	0.70	0.23	6.84	12.0
1972	2.23	0.15	0.79	−0.16	0.36	2.8	0.69	0.19	6.89	12.9

Year	GNP	Transfer	Foreign debt	Balance payments	Reserves	Unemployment	Expenditures	Defense expenditures	Family income	Inflation
1973	2.26	0.24	0.77	−0.30	0.43	2.6	0.91	0.38	6.53	20.0
1974	2.24	0.13	0.66	−0.26	0.25	3.0	0.81	0.28	6.54	39.7
1975	2.27	0.18	0.87	−0.34	0.30	3.1	0.95	0.32	6.90	39.3
1976	2.18	0.20	0.96	−0.25	0.32	3.6	0.97	0.34	7.09	31.3
1977	2.33	0.16	1.04	−0.18	0.36	3.9	1.05	0.30	7.28	34.6
1978	2.41	0.17	1.27	−0.24	0.53	3.4	0.96	0.23	7.48	50.6
1979	2.48	0.18	1.24	−0.23	0.53	2.9	0.95	0.27	7.67	78.3
1980	2.45	0.16	1.22	−0.21	0.56	4.8	0.95	0.24	6.57	131.0
1981	2.65	0.15	1.25	−0.22	0.57	5.1	1.00	0.22	7.56	116.8
1982	2.61	0.13	1.37	−0.23	0.61	5.0	n.a.	0.21	7.46	120.3
1983	2.63	0.11	1.14	−0.20	0.45	4.5	n.a.	0.23	n.a.	207.9
1984	2.60	0.08	1.25	−0.16	0.40	5.5	n.a.	n.a.	n.a.	399.3

GNP: index of gross national product per capita corrected for inflation
Transfer: international transfers as percentages of gnp
Foreign debt: foreign liabilities as percentage of gnp
Balance payments: balance of payments as percentage of gnp
Reserves: foreign currency reserves as percentage of gnp
Unemployment: unemployed as percentage of workforce
Expenditures: expenditures of government, local authorities, and national institutions as percentage of gnp
Defense expenditures: defense expenditures as percentage of gnp
Family income: index of family income corrected for inflation
Inflation: index of inflation

1965-72 (controlling for inflation), and by only 0.7 percent per year during 1972-82. During 1979-82, average family incomes *decreased* after controlling for inflation by 2.8 percent.

Inflation provides its own disturbances to living standards, even though its statistical influence has been removed from the indicators described above. With nominal prices and wages changing constantly, families spend a great deal of time and nervous energy worrying about their purchases and savings. At the same time they lack an environment of stability to help with their forecasts and planning. Israel's annual rates of inflation remained below 10 percent during 1959-69; increased gradually to 51 percent during 1970-77; and moved further until they were above 100 percent during each year from 1980 through 1984. In the later months of 1984, price changes on an annual basis approached 1,000 percent! We return to the topic of inflation several times in this book, especially in chapter 7.

Social Indicators

Social indicators are available for numerous countries.[12] They permit systematic cross-national comparisons on a range of items that touch upon living standards. However, they suffer from national peculiarities in the ways that indicators are defined, and their sporadic availability over a span of years. These problems can be minimized by limiting the range of national comparison. Here the focus will be on the pairing of the United States and Israel, chosen largely on the basis of the author's familiarity with their data sources. This limited pairing will be supplemented by a number of social indicators available on a one-time basis for 15 to 26 Western countries. Table 4-3 shows fourteen social measures that are available over time for the United States and Israel. They are based on data corrected for the differences in the population between the two countries, and are reported as Israeli-to-U.S. ratios, for years of availability from 1950. Table 4-4 shows similar measures available on a one-time basis for the 1975-80 period for 15 to 26 of the developed, Western countries considered in the analysis of national income. The strongest conclusions about Israel's standing on social indicators will rest on findings that are similar in both the longitudinal comparisons with the United States, and the cross-sectional comparisons with the larger group of countries.

The interpretation of data such as those of tables 4-3 and 4-4 brings to the fore conflicting perspectives on the concept of living standards. The interpretations here rest on the following value criteria: that higher rates of marriage, births, life expectancy, consumption of calories and proteins, telephones, private automobiles, students in universities, and hospital beds are indications of social advantage; higher rates of divorce, infant death, murder, and suicide are indications of social disadvantage.

Table 4-3
Social Indicators #1

Israeli Rates Expressed as Percentages of U.S. Rates						
	1955	1960	1965	1970	1975	1980
Marriage	89	91	84	84	93	72
Births	115	111	132	141	188	152
Life expectancy females	99	100	100	98	97	103
Life expectancy males	103	106	105	104	103	104
Calories	80*	87	n.a.	89	n.a.	87
Protein	89*	89	n.a.	91	n.a.	91
Home telephones	n.a.	n.a.	n.a.	40	n.a.	72
Private autos	n.a.	5	n.a.	19	n.a.	n.a.
Students in universities	n.a.	n.a.	2	36	43	42
Hospital beds	n.a.	79	n.a.	100	100	112
Divorce	53	47	36	23	19	22
Infant death	138	112	103	118	142	121
Murder	n.a.	n.a.	n.a.	n.a.	13	20
Suicide	n.a.	77	n.a.	55	62	54

* data shown for 1950
Source: *Statistical Abstract of the United States, 1982-83* (Washington: Bureau of the Census, 1982), pp. 6, 60, 71, 81, 112, 128, 159, 174, 432, 751.
Statistical Abstract of Israel, 1983 (Jerusalem: Central Bureau of Statistics, 1984), pp. 75, 115, 316, 329, 626, 677, 734, 761.

Table 4-4
Social Indicators #2
Israeli Rates Expressed as Percentages of Multicountry Average

	N	Israeli Rate Compared with Group Average
Marriage	25	116
Births	26	164
Life expectancy females	25	99
Life expectancy males	25	103
Calories	26	91
Protein	26	107
Post-secondary education	24	116
Hospital beds*	26	61
Divorce	22	61
Infant death	23	130
Suicide	15	37

Source: George Thomas Kurian, *The New Book of World Rankings* (New York: Facts on File, 1984), pp. 20, 31, 33, 327, 328, 330, 334, 349, 351, 353, 370.
* This indicator reversed from Kurian's population over hospital beds to hospital beds over population in order to be parallel to the indicator shown in Table 4-3.

It is possible to quarrel about several of these criteria. A prominent dispute centers on birth rates. There are many who perceive high birth rates as problematic, if not actually pathological. However, there are several reasons to analyze Israeli data from the perspective that a birth rate higher than the Western average is a positive accomplishment. Religious tenets of Judaism place a high value on fertility. Moreover, the Israeli government pursues pronatal policies, including payments for the medical costs of pregnancy, grants for maternal leave from work, and escalating family payments to mothers with numerous children. Israelis who support such policies justify them by reference to the population disadvantages of Israel in relation to other countries in its region, and the overall decline in world Jewry from 1939,[13] reflecting the Holocaust and low Jewish birth rates in North America.

There are also people who take a negative view of increases in telephones, automobiles, and the consumption of calories and protein. In this chapter the perspective is that of many poor countries, whose populations aspire to reach the levels in these indicators achieved by the wealthy.

The data of tables 4-3 and 4-4 are complex. The following summaries describe the prominent patterns. Later analyses will deal with some anomalies that are lost to these simplifications.

Marriage: Israel has a lower incidence of marriage than the United States, and the relative incidence declined even further over the 1955-80 period. Compared to the larger group of countries, however, Israel's marriage rate is higher than the average. (The United States stands out in this grouping with the highest rate of marriages, some 1.6 times the group average.)

Births: Israel has a higher birth rate than the United States, and the relative rate increased over the 1955-80 period. Israel's birth rate is also substantially higher than the group of Western countries.

Life expectancy: Israeli females and males can expect to live slightly longer than their U.S. counterparts.[14] Israeli rates improved slightly over U.S. rates during the 1955-80 period. However, the differences between the two countries are not great. Compared to the larger group of Western countries, Israel has a slightly longer than average life expectancy for males, and a slightly shorter life expectancy for females. However, Israel's scores do not depart markedly from the comparison group.[15]

Consumption of calories: Israelis consume fewer calories per day than Americans, but increased their relative consumption over the 1950-80 period. Israelis also consume fewer calories per day than the average among Western countries.

Consumption of protein: Israelis consume less protein per day than Americans, but increased their relative consumption slightly over the 1950-80 period. Israelis consume more protein per day than the average among Western countries.

Homes with telephones: Israel remains far behind the United States, although its relative position increased substantially during the 1970-80 period.

Families with private autos: Israel remains far behind the United States, although its
relative position increased substantially over the period 1960-70.

Students in universities: Israel remains far behind the United States, although its
relative position increased substantially over the 1965-80 period.[16] Israel
scores ahead of the multicountry average on students enrolled in postsecond-
ary education.

Incidence of hospital beds: Israel moved from a position relatively behind to relatively ahead of the United States over the 1960-80 period. Israel and the
United States score below the Western country average on a similar indicator.

Incidence of divorce: Israel's divorce rate is substantially lower than that of the
United States, and declined even further relative to the United States over the
1955-80 period. Israel's divorce rate is also substantially below the average of
Western countries.

Incidence of infant death: Israel's rate is higher than that of the United States, and
alternately decreased and increased relative to that of the United States over
the 1955-80 period. Israel's infant death rate is also substantially above the
average of Western countries.

Incidence of murder: Israel's rate is substantially lower than that of the United
States, although it increased somewhat toward the United States rate over the
1975-80 period.

Incidence of suicide: Israel's rate is substantially lower than that of the United
States, and declined even further relative to the United States over the
1960-80 period. Israel's rate is also substantially below the average of Western
countries.[17]

Subnational Differences in Living Standards

Among the tricky issues in the analysis of living standards is that of
population subgroups. Not only is the Israeli population made up of Jews
and non-Jews but the Jewish majority (83 percent) is itself divisible into
Jews from "Eastern" and "Western" backgrounds. Each of these classifications has significance for living standards. Ethnicity is prominent enough
in Israel so that the Central Bureau of Statistics reports some of its data
only for Jews and non-Jews, and not for the population overall.[18] Ethnicity
is well known as an important variable within the United States.

The indicator of infant mortality reveals some of the differences in living
standards between distinctive population groups in both Israel and the
United States. Jewish infant mortality has generally been about 80 percent
the overall Israeli rate since 1955. Within the United States, the infant
mortality of whites has been about 88 percent of the overall rate. Over the
1955-80 period, Jewish infant mortality in Israel declined by 62 percent;
all-Israeli, by 59 percent. Comparing Jewish infant mortality for Israel with
white infant mortality for the United States reveals that the comparison
favors the United States, although not as strongly as the comparisons of the
overall national indicators as shown in table 4-4.[19]

Analysis

Israel's living standards have performed well in relation to those of the United States and other Western countries as measured by present rates or relative growth in a number of social indicators: birth rates, divorce, murder, suicide, university students, telephones, and automobiles. There are weaker findings for Israeli advantages in male life expectancy and the daily consumption of calories and protein. Israel's living standards show continuing disadvantages as measured by rates of infant mortality. Israel's national income per capita increased in the two decades after 1960, although its income in relation to a group of some two dozen other countries decreased.

How to explain Israel's relative decline in national income per capita, and its success in various social indicators? In regard to the relative decline in national income per capita, part of the explanation lies with the rapid growth after 1960 shown by other countries, especially those of Western Europe and Japan. They suffered directly from World War II, and increased their economic standings from an abnormally low postwar though that still existed in 1960.

Israel's own history also helps to explain its relative declines in national income per capita. Through much of its early years Israel benefited from financial restitutions from the West German government, donations from world Jewry, and aid from other governments that produced especially high rates of foreign assistance. Net international transfers reached peaks in relation to Israeli GNP during the middle 1950s that were not to be repeated until another wave of external aid followed the Yom Kippur War of 1973.[20]

Israel was still in its period of massive building in 1960. Projects to construct housing, roads, and other public works were the local manifestations of the financial aid that flowed to Israel from overseas, and added to the incomes of local workers, contractors, and suppliers of raw materials. Also, the waves of refugees that arrived in the late 1940s and early 1950s represented a pool of human capital that could be developed economically.[21] Perhaps after an initial spurt of Israeli material and human development—which peaked about 1960—the country settled to its "natural" place in the economic order of things, somewhere near the bottom of the nations thought of as "Western" and/or "developed."

Economic events surrounding the 1973 Yom Kippur War were especially severe in their influence on the later years of the 1960-80 period. Of all Israel's wars after 1948, the war of 1973 was the costliest in terms of human and financial losses. The early Egyptian and Syrian successes during the war also added to Israelis' sense of vulnerability, and prompted the government to an unprecedented—and expensive—postwar period of stockpiling military hardware and petroleum. Also as a result of the war, the civilian economy suffered from a lengthy period of mobilization of the military reserves, and a marked drop in the rate of immigration. Each of these events influenced the signs of economic decline apparent for 1970-80 in table 4-1.

The explanation of Israel's positive scores in various social indicators reflects a combination of Israel's stage of economic development, its religious and cultural values, and its international environment. Like other poor countries, Israel began the 1960-80 period with especially low scores on such indicators as home telephones, private autos, university education, and the consumption of calories and protein. The signs of catching up relative to the United States, which appear in table 4-3 for Israel, are likely to be shown for a number of other developing countries as well.

The religious and cultural values of Israelis help to explain the relatively low scores of the country on such indicators as divorce, murder, and suicide; its high scores on birth rates; and the scores for higher education. Israel has shown a sharp increase in higher education with respect to the United States, and ranks above the average shown for a group of Western countries on a parallel indicator.

Israel's international setting, with the strong emphasis on national defense, frequent wars, and widespread participation in the armed services may provide outlets for personal aggression, and help to explain the low scores on murder and suicide. The indication in table 4-3 of an increase in murder rates between 1975 and 1980 may reflect Israel's maturation as a more normal, secular society.

Infant mortality is the one social indicator available for this analysis where Israel shows distinct disadvantages with respect to the United States and a group of Western countries. The difference persists, even while it is lessened, when the comparison rests on infant mortality rates for Israeli Jews alone.[22] Over the 1955-80 period the all-Israeli rate has declined more than the rate for the United States, but the decline has not been consistent within that time frame. The data for 1975, in particular, show a sharp increase in the Israeli infant death rate with respect to that of the United States. Israel's rate declined again in the 1975-80 period, but did not reach the level achieved—relative to the United States—in 1965.

Israeli health personnel assert that their country's publicly financed health care has been sufficient to deal with many causes of infant death, but concede that it does not have the same success in dealing with the more difficult residual causes. In particular, Israel has lagged behind the United States in the treatment of severely undeveloped preterm babies.

It is a shortcoming of this analysis that it does not deal with war as a negative component of living standards. The issue is sufficiently complicated to require separate treatment. The extremity of the defense pressure on Israel makes comparison with any other contemporary Western society tenuous.

There are no simple and unambiguous conclusions in such matters as national standards of living. Few social or economic traits are measured in a comparable manner over time across national boundaries. National variations in the way measurements are defined, and gaps in the available data during certain periods complicate the analysis further. In the clouded picture that emerges, there are both encouraging and worrisome signals for Israelis. The country's social indicators show several advantages in comparison to the United States and other Western nations. In some indicators, Israel's scores are more desirable than those of other countries. In other indicators, Israel shows impressive progress toward the Western norms. However, measures of income have declined in relation to those of other nations, even after taking steps to account for the large size of the Israeli government, and its social services and price subsidies. A review of the country's recent economic history suggests that its governments have not sufficiently recovered from the shocks associated with the Yom Kippur War in 1973 to find a path to economic stability or growth. Later chapters will return to this troublesome finding, in several attempts to probe its significance, and the responses of policy-makers.

Notes

1. Australia, Austria, Belgium, Canada, Denmark, Finland, France, Greece, Iceland, Ireland, Italy, Japan, Luxembourg, Malta, the Netherlands, New Zealand, Norway, Portugal, South Africa, Spain, Sweden, Switzerland, the U.K., the U.S., and West Germany.
2. Moshe Syrquin, "Economic Growth and Structural Change in Israel: An International Perspective" (Jerusalem: Falk Institute, 1984).
3. *Statistical Yearbook, 1981*, (New York: United Nations, 1982), p. 89.
4. "Comparison of National Accounts Aggregates Between Israel and the European Community" (Eurostat B3 Luxembourg, August 1984) (Draft). See also Syrquin, "Economic Growth and Structural Change in Israel."
5. The countries employed in the comparison are the same as those noted above, depending on data availability for the years considered.
6. Also because of problems of data availability, the measures used for government expenditures are the conventional ones as reported by the United Nations, and not the more comprehensive versions described in the previous chapter.
7. Even popular treatments have grasped this point. See, for example, articles and data lists pertaining to U.S. cities, like "Cities with Most Cities with Least," *U.S. News and World Report*, December 27, 1982-January 3, 1983, pp. 10-11.
8. See, for example, Eleanor Bernert Sheldon and Howard E. Freeman, "Notes on Social Indicators: Promises and Potential," *Policy Sciences* 1 (Spring 1970): 97-111.

9. See George Thomas Kurian, *The New Book of World Rankings* (New York: Facts on File, 1984), pp. xiff.
10. The measure of government spending is the total reported for the government, local authorities, and national institutions. The concept is explained in chapter 3.
11. Eitan Berglas, "Defense and the Economy" (Jerusalem: Falk Institute, 1983).
12. See, for example, Kurian, *The New Book of World Rankings.*
13. From 16 million in 1939 to 13 million in 1982 as shown in the *Statistical Abstract of Israel, 1983* (Jerusalem: Central Bureau of Statistics, 1984), p. 33.
14. Israel does not count military deaths that occur in peak war periods in calculating its rates of life expectancy.
15. The Israeli data that are compared with United States data are available for Jews only. It is not clear from the sources whether the Israeli data included in table 4-4 refer to Jews alone or to the entire population.
16. There is a problem in comparing all U.S. institutions of higher education with Israeli universities. The problem is minimized by limiting the U.S. side of the comparison to 4-year institutions.
17 The Israeli data available for comparison with the United States are for Jews only. It is not clear from the sources whether the Israeli data included in table 4-4 are for Jews only or for the entire population.
18. For example, measures of life expectancy and suicide.
19. Ratios between Jewish infant mortality in Israel and white infant mortality in the U.S. are 1960, 1.10; 1965, .97; 1970, 1.05; 1975, 1.06; 1979, 1.18. Sources: *Statistical Abstract of Israel, 1983*, p. 76; *Statistical Abstract of the United States, 1982-83*, p. 75.
20. Net foreign transfers as percentages of Israeli GNP were 1952, 6; 1955, 18. See table 4-2 for each year from 1959.
21. Jacob Metzer, "The Slowdown of Economic Growth in Israel: A Passing Phase or the End of the Big Spurt?" and Nadev Halevi, "The Structure and Development of Israel's Balance of Payments," both published by the Falk Institute, Jerusalem, 1983.
22. This comparison is not available within the framework of the data shown in table 4-3 for the group of Western countries.

5

Israeli Municipalities: Local Initiative
Amidst Central Controls

The local authorities of Israel resemble the irresistible force that encounters an immovable object. The immovable object is the seemingly rigid centralization of power in the hands of central government ministries. The irresistible force is the entrepreneurial seeking after opportunity that occurs in local authorities as well as in other parts of the Israeli establishment.[1] In reality, neither the irresistible force of local authority entrepreneurs nor the immovable object of central government ministries lives up to extreme expectations. Aggressive local authorities and strong government ministries manage to survive alongside one another. The underlying strengths of the opposing forces, the arrangements worked out between them, and the results in terms of resource distribution are important features of Israel's policy-making and program implementation.[2]

Israeli Local Authorities

Israel is a highly urban society, with 67 percent of its residents living in 93 communities with over 5,000 population. About two-thirds of municipal revenues come from central government grants, and one-third from locally collected taxes and service charges. The principal consumers of these resources are education (26 percent), development projects (16 percent), general administration (12 percent), sanitation (8 percent), welfare (8 percent), and culture (6 percent).

National power rests with the Knesset and national ministries. There are basic laws that can be changed only with an extraordinary majority of the Knesset, but there is no written constitution to block initiatives that have strong support in the Knesset. The Interior Ministry wields the power of approval or denial over local physical planning, and shares the financial control of local councils with the Finance Ministry. These ministries determine each year's general grants to local authorities. The Finance Ministry also has budgetary control over special purpose grants that flow from other ministries to local authorities. The Interior and Finance ministries govern the taxes and service charges that localities can levy on their residents, and—at least formally—they control the access of localities to bank loans.

The political culture of Israel reinforces the centralization that appears in its formal structures. There are few regional or local social attachments, partly because the society is new in Israel.[3] The single house Knesset reflects the lack of regionality: its members are chosen according to proportional representation in a single national constituency. The major political parties make some effort to select candidates from each major region and city, but there are no formal representatives from districts or communities.

Personnel in national ministries express attitudes that both reflect and bolster centralization. They tend to view authority as resting in national hands, with ministries having the option, at their convenience, of granting some of it to localities. Some of them express concern about the competence of local officials. Some support the transfer of greater authority to local officials. However, their support is likely to be justified on grounds of administrative convenience and efficiency rather than any fundamental sense of local autonomy. The recommendations of a prestigious national commission urged greater financial independence for local authorities;[4] however, these recommendations remain unimplemented more than three years after being presented to the government.

Alongside this image of a strong central government are numerous local authorities that demand, and receive, special treatment.[5] National financial aids to localities operate on the basis of formulae, but the formulae recognize the peculiarities of local conditions, and provide room for special appeals.[6]

The entrepreneurs who govern some of Israel's localities exploit what seem to be their special circumstances.[7] Jerusalem's mayor emphasizes his city's status as the national capital and the religious center of world Jewry. Tel Aviv's mayor plays on his city's importance in the country's largest metropolitan area, and as the country's financial, commercial, and cultural center. The mayors of several small, poor, "development towns" seek special grants on the basis of their residents' misfortunes, and the needs to improve housing, health, educational, and recreational facilities. Observers believe that mayors who have political party ties with national government ministers are better off than others in the competition for resources.[8]

Issues of Method and Measurement

Israel is a country that requires subset analyses of its local authorities. The most obvious division is that which separates the large Jewish sector (83 percent of the population in 1982) from the Arab minority. There are 27 Arab communities of over 5,000 population within the pre-1967 borders of Israel. Nazereth (45,000) is the only Arab settlement with more than 25,000 residents. The 27 Arab local authorities considered in this analysis account—in the aggregate—for only 6.6 percent of the nation's population. The remainder of Israel's Arab population lives in mixed Jewish-Arab cities that are largely Jewish in their population (e.g. Jerusalem, Haifa, Tel Aviv-Yafo, Acco, Ramla), or in villages that are smaller than 5,000 population. The Arab and Jewish communities in the occupied territories are subject to a combination of Jordanian and military law. They are outside the scope of this chapter.

Even those Arab communities with several thousand residents present the impression of being villages. Buildings are set here and there amidst twisting streets or paths instead of in the orderly blocks of the Jewish cities. Only Nazereth and Shfaram in the Arab sector have municipal status. The remaining Arab communities make do with the lesser powers of "local councils."

Arab communities are poorer than their Jewish counterparts. According to the economic indicator of private autos per 1,000 residents,[9] Arab communities over 5,000 population score only 32 percent as high as their Jewish counterparts. The Arab sector is also marked by a reluctance and/or inability to pay taxes and service charges. In part this reflects a larger reluctance to support institutions associated with the Jewish state. It also reflects the reluctance of central government authorities to compel Arab local councils to collect at least the minimum local taxes that are required of local councils in the Jewish sector. The income per capita generated from local taxes and service charges of Arab authorities over 5,000 population was only 27 percent that of Jewish communities in 1981-82. Reports of the state comptroller typically cite the lack of trained staff in Arab municipalities, and the faulty management of finances and other public matters.[10] The typical head of an Arab community is less aggressive than his Jewish counterpart. Taken as a whole, however, the Arab sector can pose a substantial nuisance via demonstrations televised in Israel and overseas that assert unequal treatment.

There are also sectorial differences among communities within the Jewish sector.[11] Most prominent are those involving economic resources and ethnicity, which vary together. Lower-income communities have a high incidence of Oriental Jews from Asia and Africa.[12]

The principal task of this chapter is to array Israel's local authorities according to their success in raising revenues amidst the formal structure of strong central government control. For this purpose, a summary index of *financial prowess* was devised that includes several indicators of financial success by local authorities. The data for these and other indicators come from the Interior Ministry and the Central Bureau of Statistics. The local authorities considered are all those with at least 5,000 population.[13]

The index of financial prowess is composed of the following:

- total budget per capita (i.e. the sum of the operating and the development budget);[14]
- central government aid as a percentage of the operating budget; and
- deficit per capita accumulated over the course of several years to 1981-82.

The index of financial prowess equals the sum of each authority's score on each of the above components, with the authority's score on each component first computed as a percentage of all authorities' average on that component.

Financial prowess reflects success in achieving a high budget, with a high share of central government participation. A sizable accumulated deficit is also a sign of prowess. Sooner or later, the Finance Ministry is likely to provide special loans or grants that will pay off the deficit. Components of the summary measure of financial prowess correlate moderately with one another within the Jewish sector,[15] but not within the Arab sector.[16]

Additional analyses were made with the following dependent variables:

- government aid per capita; and
- locally raised taxes and service charges per capita.

Separate analyses were made for the Arab and Jewish communities, using the following independent variables:

- incidence of private autos per 1,000 population;
- incidence of Oriental Jews (used among the Jewish communities only);
- population;
- population growth 1972-82; and
- population growth 1978-82.

The purposes of the analysis were to identify general patterns of resource allocation, and to identify and explain individual communities that depart markedly from the general trends of resource allocation that are associated with their socioeconomic characteristics. Distinctive communities were identified by comparing their true scores on the measure of financial prowess with the score predicted for them on the basis of regression analysis. This analysis of distinctive communities was limited to the Jewish sector. The regression analysis found most efficient for this purpose included the percentage of Oriental Jews and population as the independent variables.

There was a national election in Israel during 1981, coinciding with the period covered by this analysis. It is likely that the political-business-cycle

behavior of the finance minister affected the overall level of central government aid to localities, as well as its distribution to individual communities,
and the central government's tolerance for local authorities' deficits.[17]

Findings: Variations among Local Authorities

Despite the strong formal powers that reside in the hands of central
government ministries, local authorities demonstrate a substantial amount
of variation in their financial activities. Table 5-1 shows variations between
the highest and lowest scores that range upward from a factor of 2 to 1, to
14 to 1 and beyond in both the Arab and Jewish sectors. Variations by
themselves do not indicate local initiative. Several of the general finding
reflect the policy of redistribution from less-needy to more-needy secto
that is built into government formulae used to aid local governmen
However, individual localities stand out over and above what is expect
from the general model of redistribution. In the context of what is kno
about the permissiveness shown in Israel toward entrepreneurial local officials, the data go far in suggesting the presence of local initiative.

Findings: Financial Prowess in Jewish and Arab Sectors

The policy game is different in the Jewish and Arab sectors. T
apparent in the analysis of financial prowess, as well as the other featres
local activity and national-local relations considered here. The su
measure of financial prowess is 2.4 times higher for Jewish comr
than for Arab communities. One component of that summary m su
the per capita total of operating and development budgets—ave
times higher in Jewish communities than in Arab communities
component of the summary measure is the per capita deficit acc n t
to 1981-82: 51 of 66 Jewish communities had accumulated a
then, while only one of 27 Arab communities (Nazereth) had ac
a deficit. The third component of the summary measure is the per tage
of government aid in the operating budget: this is 9 percent hi Arab
than in Jewish communities.

There are also Jewish-Arab differences in the *types of com ur es* that
show more or less financial prowess. Prowess is distributed " sively"
in the Jewish sector, and "regressively" in the Arab sector. A own in
table 5-2, Jewish communities that score well on the summary measure of
financial prowess, as well as its components, tend to be poor, Oriental in
their social composition, and small in population. Among Arab communities, in contrast, it is the relatively well-to-do that score highest on the
summary measure of financial prowess. Government aid as a percentage of

Table 5-1
Measures of Central Tendency and Dispersion

	Mean	Standard deviation	Ratio of highest to lowest score
Jewish Sector: N = 64 or 61#			
Summary measure of			
financial prowess	3.56	1.70	6.31:1
Total budget/capita	5429	1734	3.34:1
Accumulated deficit/capita	410	415	1836:0
Govt aid as % of			
regular budget	.61	.16	2.84:1
Govt aid/capita	2834	1372	6.85:1
Income/capita raised			
locally	1247	564	7.93:1
Arab Sector: N = 27			
Summary measure of			
financial prowess	1.49	.26	2.22:1
Total budget/capita	1561	585	4.49:1
Accumulated deficit/capita	x	x	257:0
Govt aid as % of			
regular budget	.71	.12	2.07:1
Govt aid/capita	925	388	8.85:1
Income/capita raised			
locally	303	232	14.04:1

Notes: Indicators are as of Israeli financial year 1981/82.
Per capita data are shown in shekels.
The "Jewish sector" includes communities whose populations are largely Jewish, although some of them have substantial Arab minorities.
x only one case has a deficit; all other cases = 0.
The N used varies with the indicator, according to the data available.

the operating budget correlates inversely with economic resources in the Jewish sector but not (with any strength) in the Arab sector.

The capacity of statistical models to explain behavior in the Jewish sector is substantially greater than their capacity to explain behavior in the Arab sector, or in the combination of both sectors. Especially in the Arab sector, there is much to be learned about resource distribution that goes beyond the findings achieved in this analysis. Coefficients of multiple correlation (R^2) appear in Table 5-2.

Findings: Distinctive Jewish Communities

Statistical models do not provide total explanations. The ratios between true and predicted scores on the summary measure of financial prowess,

Table 5-2
Coefficients of Correlation between Indicators of Local Activity and Socioeconomic Indicators

	Private auto per 1,000 population	Oriental Jews	Popul-ation	R^2**	R^2***
All localities: (N = 93 or 91#)					
Summary measure of financial prowess	.03	##	− .03	.00	
Total budget/capita	.32*	##	.09	.11	
Accumulated deficit/capita	.05	##	.02	.00	
Govt aid as % of regular budget	− .76*	##	− .48*	.61*	
Govt aid/capita	− .03	##	− .11	.01	
Income/capita raised locally	.89*	##	.50*	.73*	
Jewish Sector: (N = 64 or 61#)					
Summary measure of financial prowess	− .46*	.52*	− .22	.21	.47*
Total budget/capita	− .34*	.41*	− .18	.12	.17
Accumulated deficit/capita	− .32*	.34*	− .13	.10	.12
Govt aid as % of regular budget	− .86*	.77*	− .49*	.77*	.64*
Govt aid/capita	− .61*	.64*	− .35*	.41*	.42*
Income/capita raised locally	.75*	− .57*	.48*	.61*	.41*
Arab Sector: (N = 28)					
Summary measure of financial prowess	.45*	##	.47*	.28	
Total budget/capita	.30	##	.15	.09	
Accumulated deficit/capita	x	##	x	x	
Govt aid as % of regular budget	− .04	##	− .15	.02	
Govt aid/capita	.24	##	.06	.06	
Income/capita raised locally	− .04	##	.13	.03	

Notes:
* significant at the .05 level.
** R^2 calculated with private autos and population as independent variables.
*** R^2 calculated with Oriental Jews and population as independent variables.
 # the N used varies with the indicator, according to the data available.
 ## calculated only for the Jewish sector.
 x only one case has a deficit; all other cases = 0.
 The N's for the Arab and Jewish sector do not add to the largest N shown for all localities because some data for two "localities" were for pairs of adjacent localities (one Jewish one Arab) combined. Where available, these data were used for calculations pertaining to all localities, but not for the Jewish or the Arab sectors separately.

shown for the Jewish sector in table 5-3, provide much opportunity for interviewing, document searching, and other tools of traditional political science. There are no readily identified categories that provide general explanations for the ratios of table 5-3. Population size, age of local authority, and status as "development town" all fail to correlate with the findings. As befits the concept of *residuals*, these findings lend themselves to explanations that are based upon the peculiar traits of each authority. In

Table 5-3
Ranked Ratios of Real to Predicted Summary Indicator
of Financial Prowess

$$Y = 1.263 + 6.633(X1) - .00107(X2)$$

Rank			Rank		
1	2.124	Safed	32	0.893	Beer Sheva
2	2.039	Tel Aviv	33	0.879	Carmiel
3	1.941	Hadera	34	0.866	Gadera
4	1.819	Haifa	35	0.862	Dimona
5	1.689	Upper Nazereth	36	0.848	Ramat HaSharon
6	1.599	Yeruham	37	0.838	Hertzlia
7	1.587	Kiriyat Shemona	38	0.826	Rosh HaEivin
8	1.451	Rehovot	39	0.810	Jerusalem
9	1.434	Nahariya	40	0.791	Tiberias
10	1.358	Migdal HaEmek	41	0.748	Kiriyat Gat
11	1.345	Hazor	42	0.744	Ramat Gan
12	1.296	Kiriyat Ata	43	0.741	Petah Tikva
13	1.284	Yavneh	44	0.721	Nes Ziona
14	1.256	Kiriyat Tivion	45	0.716	Pardes Hana
15	1.231	Arad	46	0.712	Ramla
16	1.213	Sedrot	47	0.702	Givatayim
17	1.207	Elat	48	0.682	Netivot
18	1.178	Beit Shan	49	0.673	Kfar Saba
19	1.177	Givat Shmuel	50	0.668	Afula
20	1.164	Lod	51	0.663	Kiriyat Ono
21	1.081	Kiriyat Yam	52	0.648	Rishon L'Zion
22	1.075	Beit Shemesh	53	0.604	Ashkelon
23	1.069	Kiriyat Malachi	54	0.600	Bnei Brak
24	1.028	Afikim	55	0.598	Ranaana
25	1.000	Nesher	56	0.565	Kiriyat Bialik
26	0.964	Natanya	57	0.563	Tirat HaCarmel
27	0.963	Yehud	58	0.561	Or Akiva
28	0.938	Kiriyat Motzkin	59	0.555	Holon
29	0.937	Hod HaSharon	60	0.482	Ashdod
30	0.900	Or Yehuda	61	0.454	Bat Yam
31	0.899	Acco			

Y = summary indicator of financial prowess
X1 = incidence of oriental Jews
X2 = population
This analysis pertains to communities in the Jewish sector only

the case of the highest positive residuals, however, they share the general trait of having a local chief executive able to recognize and exploit characteristics of the community that can win special concessions from central government ministries.

Safed is a small city (17,000 population) in the North that has benefited from its mayor having served simultaneously as a back-bench member of the Knesset. This provided him with knowledge of the personalities and the procedures of the government ministries, and opportunities to promote his city's special features. Safed is substantially poorer than the national average. It enjoys historic standing as a religious center, and contemporary standing as a summer locale for artists and tourists. Safed's success reflects a wave of public works. There are new water lines, a sewage treatment plant, new roads, civil defense shelters, lighting, and parks. A report of Israel's state comptroller found that the municipality had some managerial problems in digesting all the public works. Contractors had to be sought after to return surplus payments, and the municipality found itself with a sizable budget deficit.[18]

Tel Aviv's mayor has exploited his city's status as the hub of Israel's largest metropolitan area, plus his contacts with the country's banks and his party colleagues in the central government coalition. He has been strong enough to present the national government with a number of *faits accomplis*. Despite policies of the Finance and Interior ministries to keep Israel's municipalities from enjoying independent lines of credit with financial institutions, Tel Aviv has substantial overdrafts with the country's banks, as well as debts with suppliers and contractors. The city is notoriously behind in its payment to the Finance Ministry of income tax withheld from its employees.[19] Personnel of the Interior Ministry and the Central Bureau of Statistics caution a researcher how to interpret the published data for budget year 1981-82, which show no loans outstanding to the Tel Aviv municipality: the data do not pertain to overdrafts and other debts that are not, strictly speaking, "loans."

Tel Aviv's strategy is to finance social programs and physical developments on the basis of financial credits that are not approved beforehand by the Interior or Finance ministries. Every so often the city faces a crisis of unpaid bills and payless paydays. Contractors protest, workers strike, garbage piles up, and the city's beaches are left without lifeguards. After some furor the result is likely to be a special, one-time, and never-again financial aid from the Finance Ministry to cover the city's debts and accumulated interest. In his 1983 review of the Tel Aviv municipality, the state comptroller concluded:

> As a result of the departure from the budget framework, the municipality created a deficit without planning for its coverage. The deficits are financed,

for the most part, with bank overdrafts and short-term loans. The municipality pays considerable interest charges, which create ever more serious
financial problems.[20]

Tel Aviv's mayor also argues, successfully, that his city is entitled to special
allocations of financial aid because it serves many people who live and pay
taxes in the suburbs but come to the city to work, shop, and enjoy its
cultural attractions.

Hadera (ranked third in table 5-3) is a middle-sized city of 39,000 on
Israel's coast. It was chosen as the site of a major electric power station. The
construction of the plant, plus the development of port facilities and other
infrastructure spanned the time included in this analysis.

Haifa's high score on financial prowess reflects some similarities to Tel
Aviv. Haifa is also a metropolitan center, and claims extra resources for the
services provided to daily commuters. It also runs up overdrafts in the
banks, and debts to contractors. Such creditors will cooperate with a sizable city (ranking third in population after Jerusalem and Tel Aviv) on the
assumption that the government will not allow the city to default.

The chief executives of Upper Nazereth, Yeruham, and Kiriyat
Shemona have exploited their status as poor development towns, as well as
additional special traits. Upper Nazereth benefits from being next to Israel's largest Arab settlement. It receives support from a government that
wants to create attractive settlements for Jews in the northern region.

Kiriyat Shemona has benefited financially from its exposed position
close to the border with Lebanon. During 1981 repeated rocket attacks
produced frequent television pictures of children crowded into bomb shelters, and interviews with city officials who described the pressures on the
city and its lack of resources. According to one cynic, "The government
paid dearly for every katusha that fell on the city."

Yeruham is the smallest and poorest of these communities. It is an
isolated town of fewer than 7,000 residents in Israel's southern Negev des-
ert. In response to a scandal in local management, the Interior Ministry
suspended Yeruham's council, and sent one of its professionals to manage
the authority. He brought personal knowledge of how ministries provide
aid to localities, as well as a publicist's sense for exploiting Yeruham's
isolation and its social problems. During his tenure the national government began a program for aiding poor urban areas, in cooperation with
voluntary funding from overseas (Project Renewal). Yeruham's miseries
qualified it for inclusion on the country's list of most serious problems, and
substantial inputs to its development budget.

Jerusalem's score of .81 on table 5-3 indicates that its financial prowess is
lower than expected on the basis of its socioeconomic traits; this may reflect

the limited nature of the indicator for financial prowess. The indicator is made up of revenues and expenditures of the municipality, per se. Jerusalem enjoys many facilities that are supported via private donations recruited by its entrepreneurial mayor for the Jerusalem Foundation. This is a private body that he established to exploit the city's attractions to potential contributors from overseas.[21] The mayor is also successful in recruiting direct central government expenditures for projects in Jerusalem that do not touch the budget of the municipality. In recent years Jerusalem profited from public building and programming in the fields of housing, education, water lines, roads, and garbage disposal paid for by government ministries and other public bodies.[22] There was also extraordinary funding for industrial projects established in the city, which the state comptroller criticized for departing from established funding procedures.[23]

At the bottom of table 5-3, also scoring lower than expected on financial prowess, are Holon, Ashdod, and Bat Yam. Recent growth there has produced inflows of local revenue via construction taxes that may obviate the need for sizable government aid or deficits. Ashdod and Bat Yam were among the small number of Jewish communities without any accumulated deficit during the 1981-82 financial year, and Holon ranked fiftieth out of 66 Jewish communities on this indicator.

Findings: Central Government Aid and Local Self-Support

Which communities are more likely to support themselves? and *Which receive the most generous allotments of central government aid?* are questions whose answers reveal something about the distribution of effort and resources in Israel. The answers are complicated, and depend on the concepts and measurements that are used.

With regard to a simple measure of locally raised finances (taxes and service charges) per capita, it appears that communities in the Jewish sector make some four times the local effort of communities in the Arab sector (shown as 1245 and 303 in table 5-1). But this calculation overlooks Jewish-Arab differentials in economic wherewithal. The measure of effort calculated as local raised taxes and service charges per locally registered auto shows that Jewish and Arab sectors make about the same effort (15,205 for the Jewish sector; 15,169 for the Arab sector). If we can assume that the crude measure of economic wherewithal via private autos per 1,000 population *understates* the differential between Jewish and Arab communities (Arab autos are likely to be older), then Arab councils may raise more resources locally via taxes and service charges in relation to available resources than their Jewish counterparts.

Indications of central government aid also vary with the measure employed. On a per capita basis, Jewish communities benefit three times as much as Arab communities (2,855 vs 925 in table 5-1). When central government aid is measured as a percentage of the local authorities' operating budgets, however, Arab communities do better than Jewish communities (71 percent vs 61 percent in table 5-1). Especially in the Jewish sector, aid tends to be distributed inversely in relation to local resources (where local resources are measured by the incidence of private autos, or by the resources that are raised by local authorities via taxes and service charges).[24] An examination of real vs predicted values for government aid received among the Jewish communities reveals that Tel Aviv appears again as a financial performer that scores substantially higher than predicted on the basis of its socioeconomic traits.

Discussion

When the irresistible force of Israel's public-sector enterpreneurialism—expressed among local authorities—comes up against the immovable object of strong formal centralization, it is possible to see movement on the part of both dominant and contrary forces. There are substantial variations from one locality to the next—within both the Jewish and Arab sectors—in the indicators of local authorities' financial prowess and resources collected locally. Prominent on the lists of the financially successful are a number of the locales featured in the stories that circulate among Israel's policymakers and policy-watchers: Tel Aviv plus a number of smaller, distressed communities whose leaders take advantage of their miseries in pressing the government for extra funds. Jerusalem is not prominent according to the measures of financial success considered here. Jerusalem's success is expressed in other ways: via funds that flow through voluntary channels to local bodies; and central government funds that flow directly to projects in the capital without leaving their traces on the budget of the municipality. Jerusalem's entrepreneurial mayor helps to recruit many of these projects.

Local authorities' initiative is not a simple phenomenon that is similar wherever it appears, yet there do seem to be common elements. Entrepreneurial mayors exploit local traits that are worth something in the political market. The traits that are exploitable differ from one place to another. Tel Aviv's mayor has polished his city's standing as the commercial and cultural center of the country, and his technique of going into debt to finance public services and facilities. The mayors of several small, poor, development towns have succeeded in exploiting the particular forms of misery that they find in their communities, and can be used with central government elites who are vulnerable to social appeals. Jerusalem's mayor exploits the magic of Israel's capital and its religious importance to attract contributions from private donors, as well as special outlays from the central government.

Although the data provided here offer some indication of local initiative, they also offer some indication of central control. The indicators used as independent variables show sizable statistical relations with the measures of financial prowess. In the prominant Jewish sector local initiative works in a *progressive* direction: *it is the poorer, socially distressed communities that show the highest scores on measures of budget per capita, accumulated deficits per capita, and government aid as a percentage of their operating budgets.* It is consistent with other features of Israeli social policy that there is a redistribution of resources. The weakest local authorities appear to be the strongest in financial prowess.

The situation of the Arab communities is more difficult to summarize. Depending on which measure of central government aid is employed, Arab local authorities either do better (aid as a percentage of the total local budget) or worse (aid per capita) than Jewish authorities. The numerical weakness of electorates in Arab local authorities and the background of Arab-Jewish relations are important here. The total population of the 27 Arab authorities with at least 5,000 population amounts to less than 7 percent of Israel's total population. There is substantial antagonism between Arab and Jewish sectors, reflecting Jewish memories of Arab terrorism, and Arab feelings of being discriminated against by state authorities. The ill feeling is expressed in comments from the Arab sector that their local authorities receive little aid from the central government, and in comments from central government officials that Arab local authorities make little effort to collect taxes from their own residents.

Notes

1. Gerald E. Caiden, *Israel's Administrative Culture* (Berkeley: University of California, Institute of Government Studies, 1970).
2. Frederick A. Lazin, "Problems of Implementing Social Welfare Policy: Welfare and Education in Israel," *Social Service Review* (June 1982): 292-309.
3. Y. Gradus, "The Emergence of Regionalism in a Centralized System: The Case of Israel," *Environment and Planning D: Society and Space*, 1984, 2, pp. 87-100.
4. The *Report* of the Government Committee for Issues of Local Control (the Zanbar Committee) was issued in 1981.
5. Daniel J. Elazar, "The Compound Structure of Public Service Systems in Israel," in *Comparing Urban Service Delivery Systems: Structure and Performance*, ed. Vincent Ostrom and Francis P. Bish (Beverly Hills, Calif.: Sage Publications, 1977).

6. Yeshayio Barzel, "Relations of Local and Central Authorities: Financial Aspects" (Jerusalem: Ministry of the Interior, Department of Local Governments, 1974).
7. Lazin, "Problems of Implementing Social Welfare Policy."
8. *Ma'ariv*, March 3, 1985, p. 13 (Hebrew).
9. The best economic indicator available for all communities over 5,000 population.
10. See published reports on Eilabun, Aarava, and Kfar Yeasif (Jerusalem: State Comptroller, 1982-84) (Hebrew).
11. A number of the communities considered in the Jewish sector actually have Arab minorities.
12. The coefficient of simple correlation (r) between the incidence of Oriental Jews and the incidence of private autos in 61 Jewish communities is $-.80$.
13. "Local Authorities in Israel 1981/82 Financial Data" and "Local Authorities in Israel 1980/81 Physical Data" (Jerusalem: Central Bureau of Statistics and Ministry of the Interior, 1983, 1982).
14. For some communities, this indicator may be "artificially" high due to one-time projects financed via the development budget. This disadvantage is balanced by the advantage of taking account of all the resources available to each local authority.
15. r(total budget, deficit) = .35; r(total budget, government aid) = .37; r(deficit, government aid) = .51.
16. r(total budget, deficit) = .12; r(total budget, government aid) = $-.03$; r(deficit, government aid) = $-.22$.
17. Yoram Ben-Porath, "The Years of Plenty and the Years of Famine—A Political Business Cycle?" *Kyklos* 28 (1975): 400-403; and by the same author, "The Economy of Israel: Maturing Through Crises" (Jerusalem: Falk Institute, 1985), pp. 30ff.
18. *Report on the Review of the Safed Municipality* (Jerusalem: State Comptroller, 1983) (Hebrew).
19. *Ma'Ariv*, November 25, 1984 (Hebrew).
20. *Report on the Review of the Tel Aviv-Yafo Municipality* (Jerusalem: State Comptroller, 1983), p. 156, (Hebrew)
21. Ira Sharkansky, *What Makes Israel Tick? How Policy-Makers Cope with Domestic Constraints* (Chicago: Nelson-Hall, 1985), ch. 6.
22. *Report on the Review of the Jerusalem Municipality* (Jerusalem: State Comptroller, 1983), p. 72 (Hebrew).
23. *Annual Report #34* (Jerusalem: State Comptroller, 1984), pp. 503-8. (Hebrew).
24. Table 5-2 shows coefficients between aid and autos of $-.86$ and $-.61$ for the Jewish sector, and $-.04$ and .24 for the Arab sector; coefficients between income raised locally and aid as a percentage of the budget are $-.70$ and $-.59$ for the Jewish and Arab sectors.

6

Who Gets What Amidst High Inflation? Winners and Losers in the Israeli Budget, 1978-1984

High inflation disturbs budget makers. When money loses its stability, the budget loses its capacity to define programming through the coming year. Spending units assert they need more resources to meet established needs. Budget officers seek to protect the treasury by hiding the extent of the resources actually available.[1] Policy planning and implementation suffers from the fog of poor information about current resources, and the programs they will support.

Israel's triple-digit inflation provides an opportunity to examine the question: *What does this mean for the resources actually made available to various units?* The answer may belie expectations. Each year's budget has looked pretty much like its predecessors, and sometimes a bit smaller in real terms, after being corrected for inflation. If there is harm to be found in high inflation, it is not—at least in the Israeli case—to be found in radically changing resources made available to existing programs and administrative units.

From 1977 onward, Israel's inflation leaped upward from its previous modest levels. Annual inflation averaged 9 percent during 1968-73. It averaged 36 percent per year in 1974-77, after the costly Yom Kippur war. With the coming to power of Menachem Begin's Likud in late 1977, inflation moved into triple digits: 51 percent in 1978; 78 percent in 1979; 131 percent in 1980; 117 percent in 1981; 131 percent in 1982; 208 percent in 1983; and 399 percent in 1984.[2] During the seven fiscal years from 1978 to 1984, budget allocations increased along with consumer prices. Budget totals increased in nominal terms by 21,700 percent.

Research into the behaviors of Israeli budget making during 1982 found competitive gaming and advantage seeking among the principal actors. Spending ministries sought to spend their allocations quickly so as to obtain the maximum value of each shekel in their budgets. They also delayed reporting income from fees and service charges to the Finance Ministry, all the while spending the money as soon as it was received. The spending ministries wanted the fees and service charges to be counted against their budget allocation at the later date, when the nominal sums had lost some of their value. Ministries complained and sought larger allocations when budget increases made according to the consumer price index did not meet their own increased costs. However, they did not complain when their own costs increased less than the increased allotments. From its side, the Finance Ministry published lower than expected projections of inflation so as to hold the ministries to lower than expected cost increases. It also delayed allocations to local authorities and to ministries so as to reduce the value of the nominal sums that were allocated.[3] As inflation rates doubled further into 1984, observers reported that budget makers' gaming increased in frenzy.

Methods of Analysis

This chapter focuses on changes of budget allocations in real terms, from 1978 through 1984, controlling for the influence of inflation. As is typical in dealing with government budgets, it is necessary to make some choices about the data to use, and how to reconcile presentations that change somewhat from year to year.

The budget includes three principal indicators for each item: the amount projected to be spent for the coming year; the updated estimate of the amount that will be spent in the current year; and the amount that was spent (i.e. actual outlays) in the previous year. In the years of high inflation, it was customary that the original budget projection and the updated estimate were increased substantially in nominal terms by supplementary budgets enacted to meet shortfalls that occurred in the course of the year. However, the price index typically moved along with—if not faster than—these supplements. The data presented in the following tables are the actual outlays for 1978 through 1982; the updated estimate for 1983; and the original projection for 1984, in each case corrected for inflation.[4]

The consumer cost-of-living indices used to correct nominal budget figures for inflation were calculated for each budget year (April through March of the following calendar year). The indices used for 1983 and 1984 were estimates published by the government, to go along with the estimates of updated 1983 budget figures and projections for 1984 that were published at the same time.[5] The indices used to correct the nominal figures for each budget year were 1984, 37.27; 1983, 16.203; 1982, 5.892; 1981, 2.739; 1980, 1.00(base year);1979, 0.428; 1978, 0.219.[6]

Some of the administrative units that were alternately joined together and separated during the 1978-84 period were combined in this analysis for purposes of comparability.[7] Some items that appeared for only part of the time frame were excluded from the study.[8] Two separate budget lines dealing with subsidies for transportation were brought together with the budget of the Ministry of Transportation. Calculations were done with operating and development (capital) budgets considered both separately and together; choosing one or another of these modes did not produce significant differences. The data presented here combine the operating and development budgets.

Reader Beware: Problems with the Data

In a period when inflation moves faster than 10 percent per month, the timing of a unit's spending determines the real value of its budget allocation. As noted above, Israel's spending ministries and the Finance Ministry played counterstrategies during the period of high inflation: the spending ministries tried to spend as much as they could as early as possible, and the Finance Ministry sought to delay outlays for as long as possible. Certain budget items were likely to be spent early, insofar as the Finance Ministry was required to make payments to them on demand. A weakness of the research reported here is that it does not reckon with the timing of outlays within the course of each fiscal year. Because of limitations in the data available, it operates according to the assumption that the annual budget data reflect an even rate of outlays throughout each fiscal year. As will be noted below, the real value of certain items' spending was likely to be larger than that shown in the tables.

It is also appropriate to warn the reader that Israel's budget does not tell the whole story of the government's resource allocations. Chapter 3 reports substantial "off budget" expenditures made by quasi-governmental authorities, companies that are owned in part or full by the government, and by other bodies that act at least partly under the control of government. Moreover, analysis at the level of formal budget categories will not reveal some shifting of resources between programs at lower levels of administration.[9] This chapter is written in the spirit that it deals with an important part, if not all, of the Israeli budget story.

Findings

Despite the spectre of high inflation and the frenzy of intense gaming between spending ministries and the Finance Ministry, the general picture of Israeli budgeting is one of stability. Once the escalating nominal figures are cleaned of inflation, the findings are *decline in real expenditures for most units*, and *continuity in the shares of the total budget allotted to most units*. For three of the six years after 1978, the total budget was lower than

Table 6-1
Budget Data 1978-84
Controlling for Inflation*

	1978	1979	1980	1981	1982	1983	1984	Change **	Change ***
President	5.9	5.3	5.9	4.5	5.3	3.9	3.9	-2.0	-33.90
Knesset	48.1	46.6	52.1	43.2	48.0	51.0	44.4	-3.7	-7.69
Members of govt	3.2	2.0	2.7	3.3	2.5	3.0	2.6	-0.6	-18.75
Min Prime Minister	63.3	50.7	50.4	37.0	54.5	75.7	40.5	-22.8	-36.02
Min Finance	583.6	545.5	553.7	439.2	499.4	424.1	404.8	-178.8	-30.64
Min Interior	82.2	83.6	73.9	58.1	62.7	64.8	57.6	-24.6	-29.93
Police	1370.6	1517.8	1470.8	1202.9	1362.8	1144.2	1124.2	-246.4	-17.98
Min Justice	196.5	189.7	199.2	159.8	189.0	164.3	152.2	-44.3	-22.54
Foreign Min	377.3	348.6	321.0	275.7	320.4	282.0	286.4	-90.9	-24.09
State Comptroller	51.7	53.6	52.3	42.3	42.9	46.5	40.2	-11.5	-22.24
Pensions & compensation	801.3	806.7	1140.8	802.2	1153.5	955.4	1009.5	208.2	25.98
Miscellaneous	426.2	465.2	468.5	598.2	721.5	258.1	299.8	-126.4	-29.66
Party support	89.8	24.9	18.1	55.7	31.9	23.4	21.3	-68.5	-76.28
Min Defense	26915.5	32474.3	30588.0	23466.7	24163.2	26102.0	20515.2	-6400.3	-23.78
Civil emergencies	135.6	124.2	78.0	66.7	65.5	42.2	21.5	-114.1	-84.14
Admin of occupied territ	395.4	86.0	295.0	241.0	223.4	176.5	155.2	-240.2	-60.75
Aid to local authorities	3639.0	4302.9	3700.0	2661.0	2637.2	2218.0	1895.0	-1744.0	-47.93
Min Education	5899.3	5792.9	5816.7	4652.9	5328.4	4613.0	4458.6	-1440.7	-24.42

	1978	1979	1980	1981	1982	1983	1984	**	***
Higher education	1011.0	1721.2	1588.2	1165.3	1067.3	1134.9	1109.0	98.0	9.69
Min Religions	343.2	306.6	253.6	274.0	398.1	383.4	330.4	−12.8	−3.73
Min Labour & Welfare	4584.0	4189.0	3337.8	2738.7	4081.8	3898.4	3704.9	−879.1	−19.18
Min Health	2484.0	3193.4	2460.5	1912.7	2353.3	1808.0	1745.0	−739.0	−29.75
Pensions for handicapped	311.6	300.0	281.0	226.2	248.7	209.5	195.3	−116.3	−37.32
Broadcasting Authority	88.4	105.1	126.5	83.1	43.3	18.1	6.2	−82.2	−92.99
Min Construct & Housing	2675.2	3386.2	3259.3	2310.5	2210.1	1791.4	1592.2	−1083.0	−40.48
Min Immigrant Absorp	111.2	100.4	143.0	174.4	157.2	134.4	113.8	2.6	2.34
Support basic commodities	3859.1	3398.9	3465.0	7245.8	4422.2	4509.4	3606.1	−253.0	−6.56
Min Agriculture	1556.0	1221.1	1158.7	875.5	881.9	693.2	587.1	−968.9	−62.27
Min Energy & Infrastruct	503.0	532.7	1389.8	225.0	315.2	256.0	221.3	−281.7	−56.00
Atom Energy Comm	139.3	119.2	111.4	88.4	82.1	79.2	80.5	−58.8	−42.21
Min Commerce & Industry	1985.4	2711.3	2258.8	2018.3	2310.7	2163.9	1796.3	−189.1	−9.52
Develop export markets	152.7	46.7	38.3	610.9	1487.1	1506.8	1792.1	1639.4	1073.61
Min Transportation	749.9	645.1	485.8	434.8	375.2	349.0	319.6	−430.3	−57.38
Survey Dept	11.6	6.7	6.8	6.7	10.4	9.1	8.5	−3.1	−26.72
Support for credit	4003.4	4114.2	4232.6	3360.8	3449.2	2561.3	3970.8	−32.6	−0.81
Debt service	26289.4	22072.9	29564.9	21418.3	29108.4	26765.7	61443.5	35154.1	133.72
TOTAL	92570.5	96471.9	99479.7	81317.7	91293.8	88953.2	116984.0	24413.5	26.37

Note:
* showing the combination of operating and development budgets data for 1978-82 are actual outlays; 1983 updated estimates; 1984 original projections; data presented are (000,000) old shekels (i.e., pre-1986)
** 1984 projections minus 1978 outlays
*** percentage change 1978-84

that for 1978. The total budget for 1983 was 4 percent below that of 1978. The original projections for the 1984 budget increased considerably, due to a major increase in debt service. Only in the case of five of the 36 units was the 1984 budget higher than the 1978 budget. Debt service accounted for 95 percent of the growth shown by those units that did grow. For 10 units, the 1984 budget was less than 60 percent of the 1978 budget. Table 6-1 shows each unit's budget, in real terms, for 1978-84, and the change in real terms that occurred for each item over the six years.

The allocations for support of basic commodities, the development of export markets, support for credit, and debt service were likely to have been spent quickly within each budget year.[10] Insofar as quick spending increases the real value of each shekel spent, it is likely that the 1978-84 declines shown in table 6-1 for support of basic commodities and support of credit were less than those shown—or even were actually increases—while the increases for the development of export markets and debt service were larger than those shown. The data reported for these items in tables 6-2 and 6-3 must be viewed with parallel reservations.

Only ten units showed upward or downward change in their share of the total budget by as much as 1 percent over the 1978-84 period. Debt service increased its share the most, from 28 to 53 percent of the total. This should not be surprising. High inflation leads government to borrow to finance outlays that increase in nominal terms. The program to encourage exports, principally through subsidies to exporters, was the only other program to increase its share of the total by as much as 1 per cent: it went from 0.16 to 1.53 percent. On the losing side the defense share dropped from 29 to 18 percent; grants to local authorities and the budgets of the Ministries of Education, Labour and Welfare, and Construction and Housing dropped by 2 percent each; and the Ministry of Agriculture, Ministry of Health, and support for basic commodities dropped by 1 percent each.

Even when the large allocations for defense and debt service are removed from the budget for purposes of giving the smaller units a chance to reveal their changing portions, the picture is one of few prominent changes. Only two more items show changes by as much as 1 percent of the remaining budget: support for credit increases by 1 percent, and the Ministry of Transportation decreases its share by 1 percent.[11] Table 6-2 shows each unit's share of the total, from 1978 to 1984.

There were additional budget movements, which come to light by examining percentage changes in each item's real budget allocation from one year to the next. Here one finds shifts that reflect political priorities, the short-term influence of major capital projects, and the statistical manifestation of small budget items showing sizable percentage changes via the

Table 6-2
Budget Items, 1978-84
Reported as Percentages of Total
(without Min Defense or Debt Service)

	1978	1979	1980	1981	1982	1983	1984
President	0.02	0.01	0.02	0.01	0.01	0.01	0.01
Knesset	0.12	0.11	0.13	0.12	0.13	0.16	0.14
Members of govt	0.01	0.00	0.01	0.01	0.01	0.01	0.01
Min Prime Minister	0.16	0.13	0.13	0.11	0.15	0.24	0.13
Min Finance	1.51	1.35	1.42	1.25	1.36	1.32	1.30
Min Interior	0.21	0.21	0.19	0.17	0.17	0.20	0.18
Police	3.54	3.74	3.78	3.43	3.72	3.57	3.60
Mn Justice	0.51	0.47	0.51	0.46	0.52	0.51	0.49
Foreign Min	0.97	0.86	0.83	0.79	0.87	0.88	0.92
State Comptroller	0.13	0.13	0.13	0.12	0.12	0.15	0.13
Pensions & compensation	2.07	1.99	2.93	2.29	3.15	2.98	3.24
Miscellaneous	1.10	1.15	1.20	1.70	1.97	0.81	0.96
Party support	0.23	0.06	0.05	0.16	0.09	0.07	0.07
Civil emergencies	0.35	0.31	0.20	0.19	0.18	0.13	0.07
Admin of occupied territ	1.02	0.21	0.76	0.69	0.61	0.55	0.50
Aid to local authorities	9.39	10.61	9.51	7.58	7.20	6.92	6.07
Min Education	15.23	14.29	14.95	13.26	14.54	14.39	14.29
Higher education	2.61	4.25	4.08	3.32	2.91	3.54	3.55
Min Religions	0.89	0.76	0.65	0.78	1.09	1.20	1.06
Min Labour & Welfare	11.83	10.33	8.58	7.80	11.14	12.16	11.88
Min Health	6.41	7.88	6.33	5.45	6.42	5.64	5.59
Pensions for handicapped	0.80	0.74	0.72	0.64	0.68	0.65	0.63
Broadcasting Authority	0.23	0.26	0.33	0.24	0.12	0.06	0.02
Min Construct & Housing	6.91	8.35	8.38	6.58	6.03	5.59	5.10
Min Immigrant Absorp	0.29	0.25	0.37	0.50	0.43	0.42	0.36
Support basic commodities	9.96	8.38	8.91	20.65	12.07	14.07	11.56
Min Agriculture	4.02	3.01	2.98	2.49	2.41	2.16	1.88
Min Energy & Infrastruct	1.30	1.31	3.57	0.64	0.86	0.80	0.71
Atom Energy Comm	0.36	0.29	0.29	0.25	0.22	0.25	0.26
Min Commerce & Industry	5.13	6.69	5.81	5.75	6.31	6.75	5.76
Develop export markets	0.39	0.12	0.10	1.74	4.06	4.70	5.74
Min Transportation	1.94	1.59	1.25	1.24	1.02	1.09	1.02
Survey Dept	0.03	0.02	0.02	0.02	0.03	0.03	0.03
Support for credit	10.33	10.15	10.88	9.58	9.41	7.99	12.73

addition or subtraction of modest sums. Table 6-3 shows these calculations.

An example of political priorities appears in the 45 percent increase in the budget of the Ministry of Religions in 1981-82. The election of 1981 had provided religious political parties with an important role in forming the new government, and the formal agreement between coalition partners

Table 6-3
Budget Data
Reported as Percentage Changes

	1978-79	1979-80	1980-81	1981-82	1982-83	1983-84
President	− 10	11	− 24	18	− 26	0
Knesset	− 3	12	− 17	11	6	− 13
Members of govt	− 38	35	22	− 24	20	− 13
Min Prime Minister	− 20	− 1	− 27	47	39	− 46
Min Finance	− 7	2	− 21	14	− 15	− 5
Min Interior	2	− 21	− 21	8	3	− 11
Police	11	− 3	− 18	13	− 16	− 2
Min Justice	− 3	5	− 20	18	− 13	− 7
Foreign Min	− 8	8	14	16	− 12	2
State Comptroller	4	− 2	− 19	1	8	− 14
Pensions & compensation	1	41	− 30	44	− 17	6
Miscellaneous	9	1	28	21	− 64	16
Party support	− 72	− 27	208	− 43	− 27	− 9
Min Defense	21	− 6	− 23	3	8	− 21
Civil emergencies	− 8	− 37	− 14	− 2	− 36	− 49
Admin of occupied territ	− 78	243	− 18	− 7	− 21	− 12
Aid to local authorities	18	− 14	− 28	− 1	− 16	− 15
Min Education	− 2	0	− 20	15	− 13	− 3
Higher education	70	− 8	− 27	− 8	6	− 2
Min Religions	− 11	− 17	8	45	− 4	− 14
Min Labour & Welfare	− 9	− 20	− 18	49	− 4	− 5
Min Health	29	− 23	− 22	23	− 23	− 3
Pensions for handicapped	− 4	− 6	− 20	10	− 16	− 7
Broadcasting Authority	19	20	− 34	− 48	− 58	− 66
Min Construct & Housing	27	− 4	− 29	− 4	− 19	− 11
Min Immigrant Absorp	− 10	42	22	− 10	− 15	− 15
Support basic commodities	− 12	2	109	− 39	2	− 20
Min Agriculture	− 22	− 5	− 24	1	− 21	− 15
Min Energy & Infrastruct	6	161	− 84	40	− 19	− 14
Atom Energy Comm	− 14	− 7	− 21	− 7	− 4	2
Min Commerce & Industry	37	− 17	− 11	14	− 6	− 17
Develop export markets	− 69	− 18	1495	143	1	19
Min Transportation	− 14	− 25	− 10	− 14	− 7	− 8
Survey Dept	− 42	1	− 1	55	− 13	− 7
Support for credit	3	3	− 21	3	− 26	55
Debt service	− 16	34	− 28	36	− 8	130

promised substantial benefits to the religious sector. Some of these promises were allocated via the Ministry of Religions.[12]

It was for the 1981 election campaign that the allocation for party support jumped by 208 percent in 1980-81. As part of its reelection campaign, the Likud government boosted subsidies for basic commodities, which increased spending for this item by 109 percent in 1980-81. The sizable boost in spending to develop exports reflects the government's concern for restraining the appearance of inflation during the election campaign. The government kept the exchange rate of the shekel from falling as quickly as the market demanded, and compensated Israeli exporters by increased subsidies. If the data were updated for supplementals enacted during budget year 1984,[13] they would likely show increases in that election year for party support, support for basic commodities, and support for exports.

Budgetary indicators also reveal the fate of items that were out of favor politically. The residents of Israel's collective agricultural settlements (kibbutzim and moshavim) voted heavily for the losing Labour party in the elections of 1977 and 1981, and the budget allocations for the Ministry of Agriculture declined in five of the six years after 1978. Allocations for the Broadcasting Authority declined in each budget from 1981 to 1984. There were numerous conflicts during that period between the right-wing Likud government and broadcasters who were perceived to be excessively critical of government activities.

The construction of a major power station accounted for the 1979-80 spurt in the budget of the Ministry of Energy and Infrastructure. Periodic percentage increases and decreases in the budgets for members of the government (i.e. ministerial accoutrements), the Ministry of the Prime Minister, civil emergencies, civil administration in the occupied territories, and the miscellaneous item reflect the statistical impact of modest changes upon small budgets.

A calculation of budget outlays according to major economic categories reinforces the finding of decline or stability in most items, after inflation corrections are applied. Table 6-4 shows a major increase for debt service, and a small increase for transfer payments over the 1979-84 period. There were substantial declines for wages, purchases, and investments, as well as in the categories of civilian and defense needs.[14]

Inflation and Incremental Budgeting

The general stability in real outlays suggests the power of incremental budget routines amidst large nominal increases. Officials were alert to the incremental concept of "budget shares" *in real value terms*.[15] A spending unit concerned to defend its budget could succeed with the argument that a proposed cut would cause its budget to fall in real terms. Conversely, the Finance Ministry rejected many appeals for more money by demonstrating that a unit's budget would thereby increase in real terms.

The finding of *real-value incrementalism* requires coming to terms with one of the issues that has troubled the writing about incrementalism: what

Table 6-4
Outlays by Economic Category, Correcting for Inflation*

	1979	1980	1981	1982	1983	1984	Change **	***
Civilian needs	12757	10284	8690	10325	8947	8715	− 4042	− 31.68
Defense needs	32685	30961	23774	24452	26321	20692	− 11993	− 36.69
Wages	13446	12827	10494	11921	8852	9171	− 4275	− 31.79
Purchases	29023	25144	19114	20286	23913	18194	− 10829	37.31
Transfers	17245	20292	20398	20832	18618	18397	1152	6.68
Investments	11159	10763	9032	9656	7362	7067	− 4092	− 36.67
Debt service	26187	33797	24779	32558	29327	64517	38330	146.37

* data for 1979-82 are actual outlays;; 1983 updated estimates; 1984 original projections; data
  presented are (000,000) old shekels (i.e., pre-1986)
** 1984 projections minus 1979 outays
*** percentage change 1979-84

Figures shown for debt service in Tables 6-1 and 6-4 reflect different calculations in the original sources.

The data of Table 6-4 do not add to the totals of Table 6-1; some items were not taken from the original sources that did not fit into the categories shown in Table 6-4, and some were recombined from the original sources. In particular, the items of wages, purchases, and transfers were taken from within the categories of civilian and defense needs are also reported in full. Thus, there is some duplication in the items of Table 6-4.

measure of budget change should be labeled "incremental," and what "nonincremental?"[16]

If a nonincremental budget change is one that increases or decreases an item's share of the total budget by at least 1 percent, then there have been few cases of nonincremental budget changes during Israel's period of high inflation. A count of year-to-year changes of that sort from the data shown in table 6-2 reveals 19 such cases out of 216 possible incidents. Moreover, 12 of those 19 cases refer to the large budget items of defense and debt service, which either increased or decreased their share of the total budget by at least 1 percent during each year.

If a nonincremental budget change is an item that increases or decreases its own size by at least 20 percent from one year to the next, then there have been more instances of nonincremental change. A count of year to year changes of that sort from the data shown in table 6-3 reveals 77 such cases out of 216 possible incidents. However, 40 of those cases occurred in small budget items (each less than 1 percent of the total budget), where a modest absolute change could produce a substantial change in percentage terms. Moreover, 20 of the 77 instances of nonincremental positive (or negative) real-value percentage change in one year were followed by a nonincremental real-value percentage change in the opposite direction in the next year. In these cases, incrementalism appeared in the long run if not in the short run.

Discussion

Sound and fury signifying nothing is an appropriate label for real budget changes in the context of high inflation. Along with price increases of more than 100 percent in four consecutive years, the real levels and distributions of budgetary resources changed little. The case of greatest absolute increase was debt service. This is an item integrally related to the inflation, via the need for each budget to include more funds than the last to repay the loans that had been necessary to make nominal budget increases. Some of this debt service (49 percent of it in the budget for 1984) was accounted for by repayments to the government's National Insurance[17] and the central bank. Some instances of lesser increases in budgetary allocations also reflect the government's efforts to cope with pressures associated with high inflation, i.e. by spending more to subsidize exports and basic commodities. For the most part, units' allocations in real terms declined, and remained within 1 percent of their total budget share.

If most units retained their share of real allocations and debt service increased its share significantly, what was the source of the funds for debt service? Defense was the largest consumer of Israeli public resources at the beginning of the 1978-84 time frame, and it contributed the most to the increasing share that was allocated to debt service. The share of real resources allotted to defense decreased from 29 percent to 18 percent, and the share allotted to debt service increased from 28 percent to 53 percent.

The finding of general stability in real-value budget size and budget shares lends weight to the power of incrementalism as a description of what happens in government budgeting. There was much competitive gaming by the spending ministries to increase their resources and by the Finance Ministry to reduce their resources, but the real consequences of most games seem to have cancelled out one another.

The subtitle of this chapter asks about the winners and losers in the inflation-ridden budgets of 1978-84. Debt service was the principal winner, accounting for 95 percent of the amount recorded as increases in real terms by those units that did show increases. Some of this was a paper chase: there were no new resources for programs while "resources" were first loaned to the Finance Ministry by the Bank of Israel and National Insurance, and later repaid to those bodies by the Finance Ministry. The single other item that won substantial new real resources was the effort to encourage exports. It accounted for another 4 percent of the overall increases in real terms.

The principal losers were policymakers and budget officers in government units who had to scramble continuously to guard their resources from erosion. After the start of each fiscal year administrative officers with budgetary responsibilities had to compete for the attention of the Finance Ministry, to assure supplemental appropriations for their units to keep up with inflation rates greater than those predicted at the beginning of the year. In some of the years considered here, the overall decline in real allocations put considerable pressure on the programmatic units to preserve as much as possible of their earlier shares. There was a frenzy of competitive gaming. Even though the practical result in terms of real resource allocations was very little, inflation imposed a great deal of work on policymakers and administrators. Their need to run hard just to stay in place may have been at the expense of opportunities to develop new programs, or to improve the quality of existing programs.

Inflation also contributed to a loss in quality control. When spending targets were exceeded or program targets not achieved, the stock excuse was "inflation." Control officers in the Finance Ministry and auditors of the state comptroller caught spending units that made exaggerated claims, or misused the excuse of inflation.[18] However, officials in these units believe that they uncovered only a small percentage of exaggerated claims.

The pervasive increase in nominal budget outlays created a fog that hindered effective supervision and control. This same fog also disturbed the private sector. Israelis in government and business are aware of the differences between nominal and real increases in wages and prices; however, the pressures of dealing with nominal prices—and the problems in projecting expected rates of inflation and thereby predicting real price changes—creates a great deal of confusion. Inflation lowered the quality of decision making and contributed to other economic problems, like a drain in foreign currency reserves and an increase in foreign debt.[19] In other words, there were significant losses that came as the result of inflation that did not show themselves in the budget allocations for government units.

Notes

1. Naomi Caiden and Aaron Wildavsky, *Planning and Budgeting in Poor Countries*, (New York: Wiley, 1974), especially ch. 3.
2. These figures show inflation on a calendar-year basis.
3. Ira Sharkansky, *What Makes Israel Tick? How Domestic Policy-Makers Cope with Constraints* (Chicago: Nelson-Hall, 1985), ch. 5.
4. If the data for 1983 and 1984 follow the trends established earlier, the early compilations will bear close resemblance to the final outlays when corrected for inflation.
5. The indices for 1982-84 come from "The State Budget as Proposed for 1984: Budget Principles" (Jerusalem: 1984).
6. Indices for 1978-81 come from *Statistical Abstract of Israel, 1983*, (Jerusalem: Central Bureau of Statistics, 1983), p. 267. Each of the indices used here was calculated to reflect inflation on a budget-year basis.

7. In the data to be presented here the Ministry of Tourism was combined with the Ministry of Commerce and Industry; and the Ministry of Science and Development was combined with the Ministry of Energy and Infrastructure.

8. The small Ministry of Economy and Coordination; and the program to compensate residents forced to leave Sinai settlements as a result of the peace treaty with Egypt.

9. Peter B. Natchez and Irvin C. Bupp, "Policy and Priority in the Budgetary Process," *American Political Science Review* 67 (September 1973): 951-63.

10. The Accountant General's unit in the Finance Ministry is not permitted to limit each month's outlay for these items to a given percentage of the annual budget allocation, as it is in the case of other budget items.

11. Because of early spending within each budget year, it is likely that the real share changes for debt service, the development of export markets, and support for basic commodities and credit were larger in the positive direction than shown in table 6-2.

12. Sharkansky, *What Makes Israel Tick?*, ch. 4.

13. As indicated above, the 1984 data show the original budget projections.

14. In table 6-4 and in the original reports there is overlap between "civilian needs," "defense needs," "wages," "purchases," and "transfers," as explained in the notes to table 6-4.

15. Aaron Wildavsky *The Politics of the Budgetary Process*, (Boston: Little, Brown, 1974), ch. 2.

16. See, for example, John R. Gist, "Stability and Competition in Budgetary Theory," *American Political Science Review* 76 (1982): 859-72.

17. A unit with its own tax revenues, which is responsible for pensions to the aged and handicapped, payments to children, and maternity payments to new mothers.

18. *Annual Report #34* (Jerusalem: State Comptroller, 1984), p. xlii (Hebrew).

19. For example, via government spending and borrowing to pay for subsidies, and to preserve a rate of currency exchange that did not reflect the true international value of the shekel.

7

Israeli Inflation: The Politics of an Economic Concept

Inflation is one of those concepts that seems clearer on the surface than it is in reality. Western governments oppose inflation like Eastern governments embrace democracy: the agreement is unanimous but the meaning is fuzzy. Politicians who commit themselves to ending inflation nevertheless pursue policies that contribute to it. A government's campaign against inflation may be more a slogan than a serious undertaking. Tolerating inflation can be easier than dealing with serious problems. Rising incomes make it seem that people are better off, and policymakers avoid fundamental disagreements about the distribution of resources.[1]

The *what* of inflation is an economic concept: the rate at which the general level of prices is changing.[2] The *how* and the *why* of inflation are likely to be issues of politics and social relations.[3]

There is more belief than proof about the causes of inflation. It is common to assert that excessive government spending and budget deficits cause inflation. This is like asserting that death results from heart failure. Both statements may be true, but neither is enlightening. The explanation of excessive spending is more relevant to those seeking to understand (and to control) inflation than are simple linkages between government spending and increasing prices. Indeed, the record of 17 industrialized countries over the 1949-81 period indicates that spurts of inflation are more likely to precede than follow spurts of deficit in a government's budget.[4] This finding questions the widespread belief that excessive government spending causes inflation. It indicates that inflation is more likely to provoke high government spending, and suggests that analysts reconsider the conventional wisdom.

The ambiguity that surrounds inflation also appears in the claims that are made for indexation (i.e. linking income, taxes, capital and other items to the cost of living). Indexation is cited both as a cure and a cause of inflation. Milton Friedman has argued that linking income tax rates to the cost of living will end the automatic increase in government revenue that occurs as inflation boosts more taxpayers into higher income brackets, and thereby limit the incentives for policymakers to encourage inflation.[5] It is more common to assert that the linkage of wages and other items to the cost of living perpetuates the spiral whereby prices and incomes chase one another ever upward.

The fairest conclusion about indexation is that it is not necessarily a cure nor a cause of inflation. Policymakers use indexation selectively. They link some transactions to the cost of living, but not others; or they link some items more completely to the cost of living than others (e.g. linking them 100 percent rather than 80 percent to the cost of living); or they link some items to the cost of living more quickly than others (e.g. upping wages every month according to the most recent price index, rather than every three months).[6]

The Israeli Case

The economics and politics surrounding Israel's inflation illustrate these ambiguities. Since the late 1950s annual price increases have moved from what is called *creeping—or mild—inflation* (i.e. under 10 percent) through *Latin inflation* (i.e. from 10 to 1,000 percent). Late in 1984 and again in mid-1985 monthly rates of inflation extrapolated to an annual basis flirted with *hyperinflation* (i.e. above 1,000 percent).[7] Table 7-1 shows annual rates of inflation since 1959. Figure 7-1 shows monthly rates since January 1983.

Inflation has been a prominant issue in domestic and defense policy. The mix of items linked to inflation as causes or effects fuels intellectual and policy disputes. Although combating inflation is widely asserted to be *the* target of policymakers, it has suffered from being less important than other issues. Several finance ministers declared that they were pursuing anti-inflationary policies while their actions were contributing to further spurts of inflation.[8] Early in 1978, for example, Finance Minister Simcha Erhlich set for himself the task of reducing inflation from its 1977 rate of 35 percent to 13 percent by 1980.[9] In fact, annual inflation was 51 percent in 1978, 78 percent in 1979, and 131 percent in 1980. Inflation is associated with high turnover in the position of finance minister. Since 1977 there have been six occupants, more than in any other senior position.

Inflation and the Structure of Israel's Political Economy

The analysis of Israel's inflation must take account of the country's highly politicized, government-centered economy. The dominant position of the Israeli government in the economy suggests its comparison with the Eastern Bloc. The strong position of policymakers there and the inconven-

Table 7-1
Annual Rates of Change in the Consumer Price Index, 1959-85

Year	Percentage
1959	2.3
1960	2.3
1961	6.7
1962	9.5
1963	6.6
1964	5.2
1965	7.7
1966	8.0
1967	1.6
1968	2.1
1969	2.5
1970	6.1
1971	12.0
1972	12.9
1973	20.0
1974	39.7
1975	39.3
1976	31.3
1977	34.6
1978	50.6
1979	78.3
1980	131.0
1981	116.8
1982	120.3
1983	207.9
1984	399.3
1985	167.3

ience to them of price increases, have been cited as an explanation for low or nonexistent inflation.[10]

Although Israel resembles the Eastern Bloc in the government's dominance of economic matters, Israel differs greatly from the Eastern Bloc in the openness and competitiveness of its politics. No Israeli political party has ever won a majority in a national election. Competition between parties that are partners in the government coalition has worked to bid up the economic goodies offered to the public, and to frustrate efforts—usually of the Finance Ministry—to cut outlays. Furthermore, norms that are shared by each of the major parties have required the extensive indexation of incomes and capital.

Also unlike the Eastern Bloc, Israel's labor unions are independent of the government, and are a source of pressure for higher wages and outlays for social services. Israel's unions are among the most powerful in Western democracies. The Labour Federation (Histadrut) not only represents work-

Figure 7-1
Monthly Rates of Inflation

#1		#2	#3	#4
Jan	83	0.084	142.8	
Feb	83	0.061	91.8	
Mar	83	0.056	82.1	
Apr	83	0.133	294.9	
May	83	0.055	80.2	
Jun	83	0.036	47.6	
Jul	83	0.063	95.8	
Aug	83	0.072	114.9	
Sep	83	0.090	158.0	
Oct	83	0.211	721.5	
Nov	83	0.152	374.2	
Dec	83	0.116	234.4	
Jan	84	0.149	360.8	
Feb	84	0.120	247.9	
Mar	84	0.107	205.9	
Apr	84	0.206	684.9	
May	84	0.143	335.0	
Jun	84	0.134	298.8	
Jul	84	0.124	261.8	
Aug	84	0.165	436.5	
Sep	84	0.214	744.1	
Oct	84	0.243	994.4	
Nov	84	0.195	609.7	
Dec	84	0.037	49.1	
Jan	85	0.053	76.5	
Feb	85	0.135	302.7	
Mar	85	0.121	251.3	
Apr	85	0.194	603.1	
May	85	0.068	106.2	
Jun	85	0.149	360.8	
Jul	85	0.275	1347.5	
Aug	85	0.039	52.3	
Sep	85	0.030	38.4	
Oct	85	0.046	64.0	
Nov	85	0.005	5.6	
Dec	85	0.013	15.3	
Jan	86	−0.013	−13.4	
Feb	86	0.016	19.1	
Mar	86	0.015	17.8	
Apr	86	0.033	42.9	
May	86	0.016	19.1	

#1: Month
#2: Monthly rate of inflation
#3: Monthly rate extrapolated to annual rate
#4: Graphic portrayal of monthly rate

ers but owns financial, commercial, and industrial organizations that account for some 25 percent of the country's work force and a substantial part of its capital, domestic turnover, and foreign trade.[11] When the secretary general of the Labour Federation sits with the finance minister or prime minister, the dialogue is likely to be contentious, and agreement difficult to arrange, even if all the participants are members of the same party.[12] The period of escalating inflation (1977-84) might have owed something to the party competition that existed between the Likud-dominated government and the Labour-controlled Histadrut.

Israel's version of the political business cycle appears in both governmental and Labour Federation elections. During the summer of 1984, for example, and again in the spring of 1985 (i.e. before governmental and Labour Federation balloting, respectively) there were waves of governmental generosity and a reluctance to restrain the economy via actions that would cause widespread discomfort.[13]

Inflation as Effect or Cause

The analysis of Israel's inflation is complicated by numerous phenomena that could be designated as its primary correlates, and by dispute as to what is cause and what is effect. Figure 7-2 portrays the major lines of analysis. The complicated picture reflects what will be described as a *conundrum* in the following chapter, i.e. *a problem without a solution.*

Alleged Causes of Inflation

A number of analysts and policymakers agree that the prime culprit in regard to inflation is chronic deficit in the government budget. This conventional assessment seems especially credible in Israel's case because the government is by far the prime mover in the economy. Over the 1969-81 period government expenditures (including those of local authorities and national institutions) increased more or less steadily from 63 percent to over 100 per cent of GNP, as explained in chapter 3. The government's deficit increased from 5 percent of GDP in 1965-67 to over 17 percent of GDP during 1974-80, and settled back down to 14 percent of GDP during 1981-83.[14]

Those who are not satisfied by the *government budgets produce inflation* formula focus on *prior explanations* of high government outlays and deficits, plus numerous alternative explanations of inflation. Explanations of Israeli government outlays typically begin with the high costs of national defense. These ranged between 19 and 38 percent of GNP during the 1970-83 period, as officially reported. Such figures *underreport* real costs, insofar as they do not take into account the losses in economic oppor-

Figure 7-2
Causes and Effects of Israeli Inflation

```
     ---------------        -----------           ----------------
     !high demands ! <------!low growth!          !bal of paymnt!
     ---------------        -----------           !deficit      !
      !!                                          ----------------
      !!                                           \/   /\
      !!    -----------                           ------  !!
      !!    !subsidies!------------------------------->!debt!--!!---->
      !!    -----------                           ------  !!       !!
      \/  \/  !!                                          !!       !!
  --------------  !!----------------------   -----------  !!       !!
  !govt expend.! !!!panicked consumers!   !indexation!  !foreign  !  !!
  !and deficit ! !!!and wage earners   !   -----------   !exchange !  !!
  --------------  !!----------------------            !!  -----------  !!
      !!          !!          !!                       !!     !!       !!
      !!          !!(+/-?)    !!                       !!     !!       !!
      !!          !!          !!                       !!     !!       !!
      !!          !!          !!                       !!     !!       !!
      !!          !!          !!                       !!     !!(+/-?)  !!
      \/          \/          \/                       \/     \/       \/
 ---------------------------------------------------------------------------
 !                           INFLATION                                    !
 ---------------------------------------------------------------------------
  !!           !!                   !!   !!          !!      !!
  !!           \/                   \/   !!          !!      !!
  !!    ---------------        -----------  !!          !!      !!
  !!    !high demands ! <-----!low growth!  !!          !!      !!
  !!    ---------------        -----------  !!          !!      !!
  !!           !!                           !!          !!      !!
  !!           !!                           !!          !!      !!
  !!           \/                           \/          \/      \/
  !!    ---------------   ----------------------   ------------  -----------
  !!    !govt expend !   !panicked consumers!   !indexation!  !subsidies!
  !!    !and deficit !   !and wage earners   !   ------------  -----------
  !!    ---------------   ----------------------                 !!
  !!     !!      /\                           !!                 !!
  \/     \/      !!                           \/                 !!
 -----------     !!              ----------------------          !!
 !debt    !<----!!              !balance of payments!          !!
 -----------     !!              !deficit            !          !!
                 !!              ----------------------          \/
                 !!<-------------------------------------------------
```

(+/-?) both positive and negative relationships alleged

tunities represented by extensive military duty.[15] Mandatory service takes 18-year-old males for three years and 18-year-old females for two years. Duty in the reserves has recently claimed upwards of 60 days per year from males in the 22-55 age range during 1982-84. Policymakers also pursue expensive social programs on the model of northern European countries, plus investments in industry and agriculture.

The low economic growth that Israel has experienced since 1973 will be introduced below as one of the likely results of inflation. However, low growth also figures as a cause of inflation; it prompts sizable government investments in industrial research and development, and subsidies for export activities.[16]

Anticipations of further inflation among wage earners and consumers also contribute to price increases. Wage earners demand parity in purchasing power. They want to make up the differences between inflation and their incomes caused by indexation of wages that is incomplete, or lagged. They also want to move ahead in purchasing power to protect themselves from the further inflation that is expected. Consumers seek to buy while they can (i.e. before they lose further purchasing power or before the government prohibits the imports of certain consumer goods). The consumers' concern to buy becomes a temptation for merchants to increase prices.

Israeli indexation is incomplete but nonetheless extensive by international standards.[17] Indexation typically is applied to upward of 80 percent of one's monthly wages (depending on income level), and to many kinds of savings. As a result, consumption has remained a powerful force in keeping inflation going. Also, indexation minimizes the public's concern for inflation, and lessens what might otherwise be a restraining influence on the politicians who create the government's budget.[18]

Contrary claims are made for the influence of subsidies on inflation. The Labour Federation has worked to preserve or enlarge subsidies on basic commodities and services. Some of this is self-serving, insofar as subsidies for health services benefit the Labour Federation's Sick Fund[19] and subsidies for public transportation benefit its bus cooperatives. Illustrative subsidies during 1982 amounted to 170 percent of the price paid by the consumer for bread, 85 percent for milk products, 65 percent for eggs, and 70 percent for frozen poultry.[20]

On the one hand, subsidies add to inflation by their impact on government outlays. On the other hand, subsidies moderate inflation by keeping down consumer prices. Finance Minister Yoram Aridor earned a temporary reputation for political acumen by keeping subsidies high during the run-up to the 1981 election campaign. He justified this by citing the shock to the cost of living index (and through it, subsequent increases in wages) that would result from a reduction in subsidies. To his detractors, Aridor was simply bidding for votes and buying time for the economy, while increasing the government's foreign and domestic debt by the loans needed to pay for the subsidies.[21]

Over the 1974-84 period, Israel's accumulated foreign debt increased more or less steadily from 66 to 125 percent of current GNP. Growing debt contributes to inflation by increasing the budget outlays needed for payments of interest and principal.

Contrary claims are made for the influence on inflation from foreign exchange rates. On the one hand, occasionally sharp devaluations of the Israeli currency (e.g. in 1977 and 1983) have boosted inflation by increasing the price of imports.[22] Although delays in devaluation keep down the domestic prices of imports and temper increases in the cost of living index, they also contribute to inflation in the longer run. They make Israeli exports unduly costly in world markets, and pressure the government to approve significant budget items that subsidize exporters. Delayed devaluation also worsens Israel's chronic balance of payments deficit, and thereby increases the country's foreign debt.

This recitation of influences on inflation is only half of the story. The other half is how inflation is said to affect each of the elements that are cited above as having influenced it.

Alleged Effects of Inflation

Inflation boosts wages and other costs, and thereby increases government outlays. Current inflation creates anticipations of further inflation, and causes inflation-producing behavior among wage earners and consumers. Inflation makes it difficult to cut subsidies, partly because the Labour Federation objects to a worsening of living standards, and partly because the government fears the spirals that will work their influence on further inflationary increases through the upward effects of subsidy cuts on the consumer price index.

Inflation also pushes debt higher, via the need for the government to borrow so as to meet escalating costs. Inflation presses government to delay devaluations to keep consumer prices low; delayed devaluations work against exporters, and lead them to demand increased subsidies.

Even though indexation is widely cited as a contributor to inflation, labor leaders and government officials are not inclined to abandon indexation when inflation rates move ever higher and threaten increased social costs. While Israel's inflation escalated into triple digits, the government succumbed to Labour Federation pressure to upgrade salaries first every three months (instead of every six months), and then monthly. In this way inflation influenced its own continuation by increasing the extent of indexation.

Inflation also lessens economic growth by distracting public- and private-sector decision makers to financial manipulations and away from more productive activity.[23]

Major Events in Israel's Inflation

Two episodes are associated with Israel's high inflation. The first of these was the war of 1973. The second was the 1977-84 rule of Menachem Begin's Likud Bloc, in coalition with two religious parties.

The Yom Kippur War of 1973 was the most costly since the War of Independence in personnel lost and the consumption of material. Moreover, the early Israeli reversals and the rapid consumption of supplies left the country with a sense of vulnerability. Throughout the mid-1970s the government built up unprecedented stockpiles of military hardware and petroleum. The mid-1970s was also the time for receiving a new generation of expensive U.S. warplanes, the F-15 and F-16. All this in the economic situation of war-induced increases in the price of petroleum, and international inflation. From 1973 through 1980, Israel's defense outlays averaged 30 percent of GNP.

Inflation and other economic problems showed themselves in the years after 1973. GNP per capita grew by only 8.6 percent (i.e. about 1 percent per year) during 1973-80 after controlling for inflation. In the period 1959-73 GNP per capita had grown an average 9 percent per year after controlling for inflation! Annual inflation averaged 7.4 percent during 1959-72. Inflation averaged 36.2 percent in the 1973-76 period of Labour party rule. It then reached triple digits during the Likud regime of 1977-84, and soared near 1,000 percent on an annual basis during the first months of the Labour-Likud coalition that began in the fall of 1984.

The combination of economic liberalism and populism that prevailed during the period of government by Menachem Begin's Likud Bloc is identified as establishing Israel's "Latin inflation." Beginning in 1977 Israelis could, for the first time, hold significant amounts of foreign currency and maintain bank accounts denominated in foreign currency. The popularity of these options created substantial liquidity that was outside the influence of the government's shekel-oriented monetary controls. Moreover, the 50 percent devaluation that accompanied the onset of the Likud's economic policy provided a substantial boost to the price of imports and the cost of living.

The two parliamentary terms of Likud-dominated governments saw four finance ministers come and go. Each identified the reduction of inflation as a primary goal, but each ran aground in a government composed of different parties and perspectives. There are populists as well as economic liberals in the ruling circles of Likud. The mass of Likud voters came from the working and lower-middle classes of Israel. Against the finance ministers who wanted to cut the budget were arrayed ministers of education, housing and construction, and labour and welfare who worked to improve their programs, or at least to guard them from cuts. Also important was the role of two competitive religious parties, which had enough votes in the Knesset to protect the government or assure its collapse. They traded their support for unprecedented government funding for religious institutions and housing developments.[24]

Israel's finance ministers were not entirely innocent amidst the elements that fed increased inflation. Yoram Aridor was finance minister during the run-up to the 1981 election. He contributed to his party's campaign for reelection by reducing purchase taxes on popular consumer items, and maintaining subsidies on basic foods and public transportation. On other occasions Aridor seemed frustrated by his failure to convince his colleague ministers to sacrifice parts of their programs for the sake of reduced government expenditures.

What is important in this discussion is not only the particular assertions about the causes and effects of inflation but the very multiplicity of assertions. The various factors are too numerous and tangled for them to be separated analytically and measured for their importance as causes or effects of inflation.[25]

This recitation also highlights the multiple roles of the government in the Israeli economy. It hardly seems possible to take one action against inflation without setting in motion a series of events that work against the action taken. Indexation provides much of the glue that holds this tangle together: a government decision to reduce its budget by cutting subsidies for consumer goods will add to the cost-of-living index and thereby add to the government's own outlays for salaries and supplies.

To be sure, not all the problems result from indexation. The already large role of the government in the economy leads claimants to assume that the government has an answer to their needs. During the spring and early summer of 1985, when the government was already preoccupied with a threat of hyperinflation and a drain of foreign reserves, it spent countless hours on the plight of a bankrupt clothing firm. The 1,300 employees of the firm found several government ministers—including by some reports the prime minister—who vowed that the plant could not be allowed to close.

Who Benefits and Loses from Israel's Inflation?

There are several answers to the question of who benefits and who loses from Israel's inflation. Commentary has focused on winners and losers among Israel's social groups, decision makers in the public and private sectors (i.e. consumers, business executives, and public policymakers), and organizations that draw their resources from the government's budget. In fact, there is no clear answer to the question of who wins and who loses. Individuals both won and lost during the period of high inflation as they found themselves in various social groupings, were counted among private- and public-sector decision makers, and benefited from various items in the government's budget. It is also easier to assert than to prove that economic benefits and losses are the direct results of inflation. The Israeli experience resembles that in other countries, where multiple roles and complex political economies confuse any simple rendering of inflation's score card.[26]

Personal Well-Being

Israelis' socioeconomic roles can be defined as membership in social class, income category, ethnic group; as wage earner, salaried, or independent; as debtor or creditor; and as dependent on the budget of one or another governmental organization. Individuals are likely to belong to numerous categories, thereby confounding a clear rendering of who benefits or loses more than others.

One summary measure of personal well-being—average family income, corrected for inflation—moved upward by an aggregate 14 percent during 1973-82. However, chapter 4 describes the limitations in measuring living standards by personal income alone, especially in the Israeli context. Also, there is no evidence that family incomes moved upward parallel with inflation: the coefficient of simple correlation between annual inflation rates and annual changes (one year later) in average family income (corrected for inflation) for the 1973-82 period is .14.

Governmental Organizations

Israel's government budget offers its own framework for the identification of winners and losers. This particular scorecard derives special importance from the government's dominance of the economy. By way of qualification, however, it must be said that Israel resembles other governments in financing substantial activities by "off budget" accounts. As shown in chapter 6, most budget items over the 1978-84 period retained fixed amounts and fixed shares of the budget, after the escalating nominal sums were corrected for the influence of inflation.

Consumers and Other Decision Makers

Along with the general picture of improvement in family incomes and stability in most items of government spending, Israelis' personal experience with inflation was often hectic. In both families and organizations there are problems in projecting economic needs. "Dollarization" (i.e. calculating incomes and outlays in their U.S. dollar equivalents) helps individuals comprehend the value of current transactions but does not help in projecting shekel prices into the future.

There were spurts of panicked buying among consumers, and much scrambling in private- and public-sector organizations intent on protecting or enhancing their financial positions. Inflation also contributed to problems of quality control. "Inflation" became a stock excuse when spending targets were exceeded, or program targets not met. A great deal of time was spent on financial manipulations, seemingly at the expense of program planning and implementation.

Policy Choices

The elements said to be associated with Israel's inflation are too many, and too intertwined to allow the clear attribution of causes and effects. The recording of who benefits and suffers is confounded by the multiple roles of individuals, as well as problems in identifying the economic and social variables that move *along with* or *because of* inflation.

Inflation has been a prominent feature of Israel's recent history, but it is less certainly the dominant or most important feature. Important in their own right are a dramatic slowing of economic growth, a persistent deficit in the balance of payments, and a foreign debt that has grown substantially in relation to economic resources. The combination of these phenomena threatens the country's economic and political independence. This is a bitter realization for policymakers who are painfully aware of historical Jewish dependence on greater powers.

Alternate Scenarios

This assessment of the Israeli government's response to inflation remains incomplete. Policymakers continue to struggle with the threats of inflation, and the cloudy picture of alleged causes and effects. They have often accepted the "essential demands" of one or another group with political clout. Other chapters detail the special demands made for ailing industries, projects of research and development, local authorities that cannot pay for desired services from available funds, and one or another group of employees that want higher salaries or want to protect themselves from a finance minister committed to cutting the budget.

The typical response of the government has been to focus on limited aspects of the country's economic problems that can be settled by negotiations or voting. There have been several "package deals" of wage and price controls, formulated in protracted negotiations among the Finance Ministry, the Labour Federation, and the Industrialists' Association. After one of these, in late 1984, the monthly rate of inflation dropped from 24.3 percent to 3.7 percent. In the following months, however, the monthly rate moved sharply upward. There also have been selective increases in taxes, designed to absorb purchasing power and to dissuade the public from expensive purchases and foreign travel.

Israel's economic problems reflected the expensive demands that are imposed on the country's defense sector, and the expensive social demands that the country imposed on itself. Responses to these demands provided Israel with an attractive society and a problematic economy. Skeptics wondered if the Promised Land had become a fool's paradise. It was asked if the country's future was to be compared with Scandinavia or Latin America.[27] The old joke about the man who fell from a tall building was told so often that it became a national epigram: as he passed the midpoint in his plunge downward, the victim was heard saying, "So far so good."

At the end of June 1985 the government met for almost 24 consecutive hours and reached agreement on yet another period of wage and price controls, plus reductions in the staffs and expenditures of governmental and quasi-governmental organizations. Elements of the new plan were declared under provisions of emergency law, ostensibly to circumvent protracted negotiations with the Labour Federation, the Industrialists' Association, and committees of the Knesset.

The first month of the new program did not pass auspiciously. One government minister proclaimed his opposition to the program, and sought to recruit supporters among his party members. There were several days of general strikes or other serious work stoppages. When employees of the Electric Company struck, sporadic power cuts imposed their costs on the entire economy. The policy of dismissing public-sector employees was especially troublesome. The Labour Federation demanded an 80-day period to negotiate the issue; one minister ordered his staff not to dismiss anyone who was a single head of family, handicapped, or a close relative of a soldier killed in service; labor leaders demanded that seniority be a prime criteria for choosing those to be retained.

Various scenarios presented themselves. International or domestic events could change the character of Israeli politics and thereby alter the reluctance of ministers to sacrifice significant programs and slices of their budgets. One such event, which periodically seemed likely, would be a drastic reduction in economic aid from the United States government. Alternatively, the fear of such draconian pressure might lead key policy makers to persist more than in the past with substantial budget cuts or tax increases.

The period from July 1985 has seen an unusual effort of Israel's policy makers with respect to inflation. Compared to the wild fluctuations of government policy and monthly cost-of-living indices that marked the period of October 1984 to July 1985 nine consecutive months of less-than 5 percent price increases may have ended Israel's experience with high inflation. The government has been tougher than in the past in refusing claimants for special treatment, and monthly cost-of-living adjustments to wages were replaced by occasional small wage compensations.

The purchasing power of wages eroded by some 30 percent as a result of the government's policy. Personnel with long service in the Israeli Police and the Israel Defense Forces, as well as with numerous private employers, qualified for a welfare agency's supplement to wages that had fallen below the officially established hardship line.

The government deliberated extensively, but did not act in behalf of the textile workers of Ata. Numerous industrial and commercial firms laid off workers, reduced working hours, or shut their doors altogether. Firms known to be in distress, or that actually began bankruptcy proceedings included recognized names in construction, shipbuilding, shipping, insurance, travel, oil exploration, electronics, and brewing. The list included seemingly impregnable firms owned by the government and the Labour Federation, as well as private companies. The seasonally adjusted rate of unemployment was 7.8 percent of the civilian labor force during the third quarter of 1985. (Average rates of 5.1 percent prevailed during 1982-84, and 3.3 percent during the 1970s.) The gross national product per capita achieved during 1985, controlled for inflation, seemed likely to continue the pattern of stagnation established during the three previous years.

Upon closer examination, however, it is possible to find the postponement of difficult issues. Public sector employment declined, as promised by the economic policy. However, this was accomplished by not replacing those who left the service, rather than by actual dismissals. The declared policy had called for greater reductions in the public sector workforce. Critics of the government also claimed that it did not deliver on its commitment to reduce budget outlays substantially in absolute terms. Israel's government remained heavily involved in the economy.

A worrisome analysis of Israel's struggle against inflation points to external factors—outside of the government's control—that contributed to price stability. In other words, it may have been good luck, rather than governmental wisdom or discipline that was responsible for the decline in Israel's inflation. The external elements included a sharp drop in inflation in Western Europe, North America, and Japan, which are the markets that supply the bulk of Israel's imports of industrial and consumer goods. Sharp drops in the international price of oil further lightened Israel's import bills. The United States government also helped greatly with emergency economic aid. These benefits from outside the country allowed to the Israeli government to moderate or postpone difficult decisions with respect to cuts in its own expenditures and workforce.

Also causing worry for Israel's economy are postponements in currency devaluation and wage adjustments. These are gathering pressure that sooner or later will be released into the economy. There has been no devaluation of the shekel since July 1985. To May 1986, accumulated price increases of some 20 per cent have had their influence in distorting the prices of foreign currency and imports. When devaluation occurs, it will boost the cost of imports and make its contribution to domestic inflation.

A period of labor peace has prevailed since the austerity measures of July 1985. There have been piecemeal adjustments granted to all workers, and additional adjustments won by certain sectors. However, a number of groups have postponed the receipt of adjustments already promised, under pressure from a government that wants to hold back a flood of demands for as long as possible.

No government in Israel's recent history has been able to withstand for long these kinds of pressures. More time must elapse before "finish" can be written about Israel's experience with rapid and continuous price increases.

Notes

1. Fred Hirsch and John H. Goldthorpe, eds., *The Political Economy of Inflation* (Cambridge: Harvard University Press, 1978).
2. J. S. Flemming, "The Economic Explanation of Inflation" in *The Political Economy of Inflation*, ed. Fred Hirsch and John H. Goldthorpe (Cambridge: Harvard University Press, 1978), pp 13-36.
3. Colin Crouch, "Inflation and the Political Organization of Economic Interests" in *The Political Economy of Inflation*, ed. Fred Hirsch and John H. Goldthorpe (Cambridge: Harvard University Press, 1978), pp. 217-39.
4. George Guess and Kenneth Koford, "Inflation, Recession and the Federal Budget Deficit (or Blaming Economic Problems on a Statistical Mirage)," *Policy Sciences* 17 (December 1984): 385-402.
5. "Using Escalators to Help Fight Inflation," *Fortune* (July 1974): 94-97, 174-76.
6. Gustav Donald Jud, *Inflation and the Use of Indexing in Developing Countries* (New York: Praeger, 1978).
7. Charles S. Maier, "The Politics of Inflation in the Twentieth Century" in *The Political Economy of Inflation*, ed. Fred Hirsch and John H. Goldthorpe (Cambridge: Harvard University Press, 1978) pp. 37-72; Richard Medley, ed., *The Politics of Inflation: A Comparative Analysis* (New York: Pergamon Press, 1982).
8. Michael Bruno and Stanley Fischer, "The Inflationary Process in Israel: Shocks and Accommodation" (Jerusalem: Falk Institute, 1984), esp. pp. 28-30.
9. Knesset Speeches, January 9, 1978 (Hebrew).
10. Richard Portes, "Inflation under Central Planning," in *The Political Economy of Inflation*, ed. Fred Hirsch and John H. Goldthorpe (Cambridge: Harvard University Press, 1978), pp. 73-87.

11. Haim Barkai, "Theory and Praxis of the Histadrut Industrial Sector", *Jerusalem Quarterly* 26 (Winter 1982): 96-108.
12. Michael Shalev, "Labor, State and Crisis: An Israeli Case Study", *Industrial Relations* 23 (Fall 1984): 362-86.
13. On the general point of Israel's political business cycle, see Yoram Ben-Porath, "The Years of Plenty and the Years of Famine—A Political Business Cycle?" *Kyklos* 28 (1975): 400-3.
14. Bruno and Fischer, "The Inflationary Process in Israel," p. 41.
15. Eitan Berglas, "Defense and the Economy: The Israeli Experience" (Jerusalem: Falk Institute, 1983).
16. Joram Mayshar, "Investment Patterns in Israel" (Jerusalem: Falk Institute, 1984).
17. See Jud, *Inflation and the Use of Indexing in Developing Countries.*
18. Bruno and Fischer, "The Inflationary Process in Israel," p. 35.
19. The country's largest provider of health services.
20. *Ma'ariv*, February 12, 1982 (Hebrew).
21. For example, the comments of former Bank of Israel Governor Amnon Gafne, as quoted in *Ma'ariv*, November 9, 1982 (Hebrew); Yoram Ben-Porath, "The Economy of Israel: Maturing Through Crises" (Jerusalem: Falk Institute, 1985), esp. pp 30f.
22. Bruno and Fischer, "The Inflationary Process in Israel," pp. 24-25, 30.
23. *Ibid*, pp. 33-34.
24. Ira Sharkansky, *What Makes Israel Tick? How Domestic Policymakers Cope with Constraints* (Chicago: Nelson-Hall, 1985), chs. 3-4.
25. See, for example, the complex and highly qualified effort in Bruno and Fischer, "The Inflationary Process in Israel," esp. pp. 18ff.
26. See the essays in Hirsch and Goldthorpe, *The Political Economy of Inflation* and in Robert E. Hall, ed., *Inflation: Causes and Effects* (Chicago: University of Chicago Press, 1982).
27. Moshe Syrquin, "Economic Growth and Structural Change in Israel: An International Perspective" (Jerusalem: Falk Institute, 1984), pp. 40-41.

8

Conundrums: Problems without Solutions

Israel is a troubled country. In early 1985 the military withdrawal from Lebanon competed for attention with efforts to restrain inflation and to stem the outward flow of foreign currency. Financial reserves were approaching the point at which there might not be enough for imports of food and industrial raw materials. Also competing for attention was the perennial issue of seeking an accord with Israel's Arab neighbors; keeping the peace at home on numerous points of friction between religious and secular Jews; meeting the demands of Israel's Arab citizens; dealing with those who fervently advocate and those who fervently oppose further settlement activity in the occupied territories; and deciding whether to go forward or to suspend activity on major development projects like the Lavie fighter plane and the water channel from the Mediterranean to the Dead Sea. Some of these issues reflect conundrums: problems without solutions.[1]

One of the traits that makes a problem into a conundrum is ambiguity. A simple problem may be solved by clarifying it. In the case of the conundrums, it is difficult to agree on where to begin their analysis. A conundrum is also likely to have numerous components, with disputes as to which are the most important. Because it is difficult to define the aspects of a conundrum, it is also difficult to find data—economic, social, or political—that can be measured with precision and used in an analysis to solve the conundrum.

Conundrums and Other Kinds of Problems

To distinguish the concept of conundrum from its close relatives, it is helpful to classify the broader concept of *problem* into its several varieties.[2]

- A problem with *one* solution. An example is a known mathematical problem. In government such a problem is presented by a client with certain characteristics, which can be matched with classifications recorded in a program manual, with the result that the client is shown to

be entitled to a fixed and unambiguous financial grant or program of services.
- A problem whose solution is not yet clear but that is under consideration and seems likely to be solved. An example is research to find a vaccine for an illness, when the illness is similar to those that have been dealt with successfully in the past.
- A problem that has several solutions. This is a typical political problem, whose solution is achieved through negotiations or voting. One subcategory of these problems is the predicament, whose alternative solutions are *unattractive*. Another subcategory is the dilemma, whose alternative solutions are *equally unattractive*.
- A problem that seems to have no solution. As long as no solution appears on the horizon, there is a conundrum. If conditions change and one or more solutions appear in sight or at hand, then the problem becomes one of the other categories listed above. A solution may appear as the result of reconceptualizing a conundrum to remove its ambiguity, or to remove one or another of its components that make a solution impossible. A political change can also affect a conundrum. Policymakers can alter their perceptions or priorities, and be willing to select options that they opposed previously. Or a solution may appear as a result of new discoveries in science or technology. While solutions may be offered for a conundrum, they must meet a certain minimum standard for the conundrum to become another kind of problem. The solution must reach a certain level of finiteness, or clarity. The solution need not be a "desirable" one. A dilemma or predicament would be a problem that offered solutions of finiteness and clarity but not desirability.

How to Recognize Conundrums

The following traits summarize the essential traits of conundrums, and help in the distinction of conundrums from other kinds of problems:

- Conundrums are ambiguous. Participants and observers disagree as to how to define the problem.
- As part of their ambiguity, conundrums are multifaceted. Conundrums are made up of different components, and it is difficult to find agreement on how the "essential" elements of the problem should be defined.
- Conundrums do not lend themselves to quantitative indicators of their components; this trait is related to their ambiguity. Analysts cannot identify the economic, social, or political features known to cause a conundrum, and therefore cannot "get a handle" on the issues, or assess the potential success of proposals that are offered as solutions for the conundrum.
- Conundrums are insoluble. This is a product of the ambiguous nature of conundrums, and the difficulties in measuring the elements related to them. Analysts cannot agree on how to define the components of a

conundrum; they cannot measure its components; and therefore they cannot measure the probable success of claims in regard to dealing with the conundrum.

- Conundrums are persistent. The same—or similar—problems crop up time and again, perhaps in different formulations or with different personalities playing the major roles.

A Universal Conundrum

A conundrum of policy analysis affects persons in any country who seek to determine the effects of policies on the social or economic conditions they are meant to influence. The complexities begin with the many policy elements, and the numerous other factors that compete with efforts of policymakers to shape the outputs of governmental programs:

1. the funds allocated by the budget;
2. the number and quality of personnel assigned to a task;
3. the quality of administrative management;
4. the nature of program clients; and
5. national and international events that affect a nation's well-being, and change the resources available for a program, or the priority that a program enjoys in its competition for resources with other programs.

This universal conundrum of policy analysis can be expressed as

How to determine the impact of "w" resource use, "x" personnel decisions, "y" organizational structure, or "z" program directives on the outputs of public policy when there are no satisfactory standards for identifying the weight of individual components of public policy (e.g. budget allocations) from amidst the large number of influences that shape program outputs?

For some of these recognized influences on governmental activity, there are no data that can be used to measure them with any degree of precision. Even where there are data of high quality, the number of recognized influences and their apparent interrelationships are beyond the power of social science to assess the weight of each in affecting program quality.[3] This conundrum keeps policymakers from knowing what to do, with a certainty that their activities will accomplish their intentions.

Israeli policymakers, like their counterparts in many countries, encounter this universal conundrum whenever they seek to decide about the influence of certain decisions on the conditions they are meant to affect. Like policymakers elsewhere, however, Israelis have learned to make decisions about resource allocation, personnel, organizational structures, or program components by overlooking unknowable and insoluble elements in the problems that they face. Perhaps because these conundrums are universal, they have given rise to evasions that are also universal. In the case of resource allocations, for example, officials vote funds for each item in the budget—often in response to pressures exerted by key politicians—without determining with absolute certainty the consequences of their decisions.

Conundrums of the Israeli Economy: Where to Start? What to Do?

The specific conundrums of the Israeli economy are more pernicious than the universal conundrum described above. Israelis cannot learn from textbooks how to deal with the particular constellation of factors that have grown up around them.

The problems presented by the Israeli economy since the late 1970s qualified as conundrums. They were multifaceted, ambiguous, persistent, and—at least until the latter part of 1985—seemed to be insoluble. One component of the problem was high inflation. A second problem was a high and growing foreign debt. A third problem was stunted economic growth. A fourth problem was a continuing negative balance of payments. A fifth problem was government expenditures that exceeded available resources. There was considerable debate about what was cause, and what was effect amidst these signs of economic trouble.

The limited question *Where to start in cutting the government budget?* illustrates Israel's conundrums. The economy is government-oriented, with virtually every sector dependent on government loans, subsidies, and/or government-approved investments, salaries, or other expenditures. There are strong components of technocracy and politics, and a minor role for the free market in the Israeli economy. Each claimant on the government's largess asserts its justice:

- An inefficient and uncompetitive clothing firm cannot be allowed to close because that would cut off the livelihoods of several hundred employees who have "dedicated their lives" to the firm and have little prospect of acquiring other skills.
- The Lavie fighter-plane project must continue, because as millions have already been sunk in research and development, the project is vital for Israeli defense, and it will retain the country's leading edge in high technology. Moreover, ending the project would result in the emigration of skilled personnel who could not find alternate employment in Israel.
- The Mediterranean-Dead Sea water channel must go forward because Jews from the Diaspora contributed their money in response to the government's commitment to the project.

- The government must continue to support settlement projects in various sections of Israel and the occupied territories, because of commitments made by previous governments and by the political parties that are members of the present coalition.
- The government must help agricultural and manufacturing sectors compete in the difficult markets of Europe and North America. Without further subsidies, the huge sums already invested in these sectors would be lost, along with the livelihoods of countless workers and their families.
- When price controls on imports and/or cutbacks in funding for hospitals create shortages in medical supplies, the government must allow importers to charge prices that depart from the agreed framework, and the government must provide additional funding to the health sector.
- When municipal authorities assert that they cannot continue essential services because the government has not met its funding commitments, and there are municipal workers' strikes and noticeable piles of uncollected garbage, the government must respond with more funds.
- Schoolteachers argue that they deserve higher salaries, within the framework of a catch-up agreement that the government accepted some years ago.
- Heads of religious schools argue that they deserve additional government funds at levels similar to those provided to other schools.

The problems of *Where to start?* and *Where to cut?* combine the detailed problems of Israel's political economy with universal budgetary conundrums that have long troubled policymakers. One of V.O. Key's early contributions to political science was his critique of the budgetary literature. He opened what became a classic article with the following lament:[4] "On the most significant aspect of public budgeting, i.e., the allocation of expenditures among different purposes so as to achieve the greatest return, American budgetary literature is singularly arid." Later in the same article, Key posed his widely quoted expression of the budgetary mission: "On what basis shall it be decided to allocate x dollars to activity A instead of activity B?"

Aaron Wildavsky made the single greatest step beyond Key, and impressed upon the discipline that budgeting is inherently a *political* process.[5] Officials pursue funding competitively, partly to demonstrate their skills in intragovernmental politics. Organizational and personal prestige compete with service goals and economic analyses as the motive forces in government budgeting. Overt politics dominate in the initial enactments of programs, and then existing commitments and routine incrementalism takes over to allocate most annual funding. Budgeting remains more in the slippery domain of politics or the frozen commitments of past decisions than in the rational world of economically oriented reformers.

The very size of Israel's government sector complicates budgeting. As seen in chapters 3 and 4, conventional indicators like GNP and national income do not offer acceptable measures of the economic resources that are available, or living standards. Policymakers in other countries may rely on these indicators to gauge what is happening and adjust government spending accordingly. Israeli policymakers risk losing touch with reality if they focus on these indicators for their country's performance. Yet, the widespread use of these indicators inserts them, regardless of their faults, into Israeli policy discussions.

Is Inflation a Result or a Cause of Israel's Economic Problems?

It is conventional wisdom that inflation is a result of governmental follies or errors. These are said to produce deficits, negative balance of payments, and a too-ready inclination to borrow locally and from abroad. Government deficits and borrowing, plus a negative balance of payments is thought to create surplus buying power in the economy, which goes to bid up the price of available goods and services. On the other hand, inflation may cause each of these evils that is thought to cause it! Increasing prices force governments to spend more to obtain a fixed level of services, which thereby adds to the budget deficit. Inflation likewise demands more borrowing to meet higher prices. The greater sums of money in circulation can add to a feeling of well-being, or the sense that purchases ought to be made quickly before things get worse. The result will be an increase in imported consumer goods and a worsening of the balance of payments.

The question of inflation as cause or effect joins the other conundrums faced by Israeli policymakers. Should they focus their efforts on inflation, or on other factors that may contribute to inflation? Or should they ignore inflation, and focus instead on other elements that are troublesome in their own right, like continued borrowing overseas and the drain in foreign currency reserves?

As seen in the previous chapter, Israeli policymakers have tended to focus on specific aspects of the inflation problem that can be settled by negotiations or voting. The government has imposed limited-term controls on prices and wages, it has imposed new taxes and increased certain existing taxes, and it has resisted certain demands for special treatment. There have also been fortuitous events in Israel's international environment. Rates of inflation declined dramatically during 1985-86. The conundrum of high inflation, per se, may be a part of Israel's history. However, other distortions in the economy remain in place, and threaten another upsurge of inflation.

Conundrums of Peace

Israeli policymakers have no shortage of conundrums outside the economic arenas. Problems that fit under the labels of national security and peace are no less multifaceted, ambiguous, and elusive of solution than the financial problems. Problems of national security and peace also redound directly to the economy via the huge sums spent on defense.

The Middle East is not only the arena of "Israeli vs Palestinian;" it is a rich collection of antagonisms between religious, national, and ethnic sectors within the larger "Arab" and "Palestinian" communities. The discrete problems of the West Bank and the Gaza Strip, occupied by Israel during the 1967 war, show some of these intertwined issues in microcosm at the same time that they reflect other issues of conflict within the Israeli Jewish society:

- Several Israeli overtures to open discussions with Arab leaders have gone aground on the unwillingness of any prominent Arab figure to discuss the sensitive issues without the hitherto-unachievable agreement of all major Arab factions.
- Indications of Israeli willingness to trade "land for peace" have brought forth sharp opposition from Israeli Jewish sources opposed to certain territorial concessions on grounds of defense, nationalism, or religious claims to the areas in question.

Lebanon presented its own conundrum to Israeli policymakers. Israel's northern neighbor is marked by numerous religious, ethnic, regional, tribal, and ideological factions, and a weak central government. The Lebanese government's tenuous control over the countryside collapsed altogether during the latest round of civil fighting that began in the mid-1970s. By one estimate there were 54 private armies contending for control over various regions of Lebanon during the summer of 1981.[6] For Israel, the problem of Lebanon was that of a government that could not keep its territory from serving as a base for terrorist attacks against Israeli civilian targets.

When the Israeli army moved into Lebanon during 1982, its intentions were not altogether clear. Government leaders initially defined limited goals of clearing a swath of southern Lebanon that would move Palestinian terrorists beyond artillery range from northern Israel. As the fighting progressed, however, Israel's forces reached the Lebanese capital of Beirut, and occupied a substantial region of central as well as southern Lebanon. Israeli government statements indicated that Israel's goals had become the destruction of the Palestine Liberation Organization throughout Lebanon. Some statements suggested the even larger goal of establishing order in Lebanon. The aspiration of some Israeli policymakers was to create a predominantly Christian government for Lebanon that would control the country's warring factions, sign a peace treaty with Israel, and establish normal relations between the two countries.

In the end, the animosity among the Lebanese proved too much for the Israelis. After more than three years and more than 650 military deaths, Israel withdrew to extreme southern Lebanon. It trained and supplied its own unofficial *Army of South Lebanon*, made of up Lebanese willing to identify themselves as allies of Israel. It was the Israeli hope that this force would keep the peace on the Lebanese side of the border and prevent the infiltration of terrorists once Israel withdrew entirely, but it was proving difficult to keep the Army of South Lebanon to Israeli standards of conduct. The Army of South Lebanon was bothered by several mass desertions of its recruits. Its troops massacred civilians in a village where they had suffered casualties. They also caused a major diplomatic embarrassment when they captured 23 Finnish soldiers assigned to the United Nations Forces in Lebanon, and threatened to kill one Finn each hour unless the United Nations Forces agreed to cooperate with certain demands.

Conundrums of Governmental Control

Even the seemingly dull and technical area of Israeli government auditing reveals conundrums that touch upon broader issues of control over the government and the economy. Government auditors face conundrums in deciding what to audit, how to examine the programs they select for attention, and how to deal with their audit findings. By being more aggressive in his activities, Israel's state comptroller may add to the government's control over its own components. Opposed to this extension of control, however, are increased financial costs for the audit body, and increased bureaucracy layered on the governmental units that would be audited more closely.

It has been some years since sophisticated government auditors—including the Israeli state comptroller—have been satisfied only to make narrow inquiries into financial accounts. Auditing has become an important part of policymaking, and the auditor has become subject to the risks as well as the rewards of political visibility. Personnel of the State Comptroller come from professions like engineering, systems analysis, public administration, and other specialties that enable them to assess the many-faceted programs of modern government. They focus on the efficiency of government programs, and the success of programs in achieving their goals.

The law governing Israel's State Comptroller is especially broad. There are virtually no legal limits to the Comptroller's reach. The State Comptroller can investigate any organization that receives financial support from the government, or in whose control the government participates. Because of the socialist traditions and the government's willingness to subsidize goods and services, the State Comptroller can reach just about every institution in the country, including banks, universities, hospitals, and many companies that are ostensibly private. The standards that the State Comptroller may use to judge audited bodies are also extensive. The Law of the State Comptroller provides for conventional checks on financial record keeping, revenues, and expenditure, and further authorizes the Comptroller to determine whether the bodies being inspected have operated "economically, efficiently, and in a morally irreproachable manner."[7]

The formal powers of the State Comptroller are among its problems. The organization can look at virtually everything in theory, but not in practice. The critical limitations are the personnel at its disposal, and its reluctance to tackle institutions that are accustomed to being outside the net of government auditing. Personnel of the State Comptroller claim that their fingers are on the pulses of many organizations, and that they look closely at those with problems; however, the physician does not visit each patient often. Government companies are seldom audited, except for the largest and most visible of them. Subsidiaries of government companies, and joint ventures between government companies and other owners are audited even less, if at all.[8]

Israel's state comptroller routinely states that he does not criticize policy, only its implementation. However, the line between an issue of policy and an issue of implementation is difficult to discern. The state comptroller of Israel has criticized some of the most sensitive issues of governmental activity. The 1983 *Annual Report* of the State Comptroller included criticisms of the government's policy to borrow overseas, and to subsidize various goods and services. Both of these items ranked high on the year's agenda of public controversies. The introduction to the *Annual Report* was a prominent place to criticize the most sensitive of Israeli government policies: the conduct of war. A day or two after the report was issued, one member of Knesset called for the State Comptroller's resignation. When the state comptroller entered a matter of high policy, he became subject to the criticisms directed at others who deal with the same issues.

What should the government auditor do in the context of limited resources and political controversy? It would be easiest to retreat. At one time, government auditors dealt only with the vouchers that ordered payment by the government treasury. Legions of accountants checked the details of vouchers against the budgets and legal authority of each department. If the paperwork was in order, the auditor was satisfied. Few politicians could complain about an officer who checked only the detailed procedures of program implementation. Although retreat would be easy, it would also entail a sacrifice of the sophistication that government auditors have acquired in recent years. Why should auditors be content with checking procedures when they can use their expertise to assess the effectiveness and efficiency of government activity?

The state comptroller also hears proposals that he be more productive with the resources already available. This throws on the auditor the same criticism that he traditionally hurls at other government offices: *be more efficient!* Efficiency is a difficult command that presents its own conundrum. The staff of the auditor—like that of other large organizations—does not move readily from its existing tasks or styles of work. There are likely to be a limited number of top-flight employees, and they are probably already working at high efficiency on priority projects. Many of the other employees are well entrenched, protected in their jobs, and unwilliing to exert themselves within the organization or to leave it and make room for newer employees. *Be more efficient!* is more often a slogan than a useful guide to improvement.

You Might Cope with Conundrums If You Cannot Solve Them

There is no shortage of proposals for dealing with these problems of resource allocation, peace negotiations, or government auditing. The issue of high inflation may have dropped from the list, thanks to changes in the perspectives of key decision makers, or because of Israel's good fortune with respect to international occurrences, as detailed in chapter 7.

Chapter 9 looks further at public-sector entrepreneurialism, chapter 10 examines policymaking by indirection, and chapter 11 considers flexibility in allowing policymaking to break some of the formal rules. Each of these devices helps Israelis to deal with their conundrums. To be sure, the behaviors described in chapters 9-11 are not entirely separable. There are elements of entrepreneurialism, for example, in policymaking by indirection, and in the willingness of policymakers to break formal rules that constrain their options. It is also the case that each of these coping behaviors causes its own problems. Some of the activities that policymakers use in order to deal with conundrums offer only temporary or partial respite from them.

Notes

1. Dictionaries agree that the origin of the word is *not* Latin. As a result, the plural will take the English form with an "s," rather than the Latinized *conundra*. See,

for example, *Oxford English Dictionary* (London: Oxford University Press, 1933.)

2. Professor Barbara Hinckley is responsible for suggesting this point and pressing its importance upon me.

3. Henry Teune, "A Logic of Comparative Policy Analysis,"in *Comparing Public Policies: New Concepts and Methods*, ed. Douglas E. Ashford (Beverly Hills, Calif.: Sage Publications, 1978), pp. 43-55.

4. V.O. Key, Jr., "The Lack of a Budgetary Theory," *American Political Science Review* 34 (December 1940): 1137-44.

5. Aaron Wildavsky, *The Politics of the Budgetary Process* (Boston: Little, Brown, 1979).

6. David C. Gordon, *The Republic of Lebanon: Nation in Jeopardy* (Boulder, Colo.: Westview Press, 1983), p. 131.

7. Law of the State Comptroller, 1958, 10, A, 2. (Hebrew).

8. Asher Friedburg, "Public Audit on the Margins of the Public Administration System in Israel," Department of Political Science, The Hebrew University of Jerusalem, 1985.

9

Public-Sector Entrepreneurialism

Entrepreneurial behavior helps some Israeli policymakers cope with their conundrums. An entrepreneur sees opportunities where others see only problems. The entrepreneur has the kind of creativity that Yehezkel Dror labels "extrarational."[1]

The concept of entrepreneurialism should be used carefully. It appears widely in professional and popular writing about politics as well as business. Its various definitions and connotations make it useful for numerous purposes, yet make its systematic application difficult in any context. The range of functions assigned to entrepreneurs reflects a composite of several roles, attributes, and skills whose mixture varies with the situation.[2] The crude efforts to measure entrepreneurialism reflect the lack of crispness in its definition.[3]

What Is an Entrepreneur?

Joseph A. Schumpeter's *Capitalism, Socialism, and Democracy* is the common source for much of the writing about entrepreneurialism, and is responsible for much of the flexibility and confusion that surrounds it. He wrote that the function of the entrepreneur

> is to reform or revolutionize the pattern of production by exploiting an invention or, more generally, an untried technological possibility for producing a new commodity or producing an old one in a new way, by opening up a new source of supply of materials or a new outlet for products, by reorganizing an industry *and so on.* . . . . (The entrepreneur) act(s) with confidence beyond the range of familiar beacons . . . The function . . . consists in *getting things done.* [italics added][4]

The specific attributes derived from such an open-ended definition include assertions that the entrepreneur[5]

- assumes risks associated with uncertainty
- is an innovator

- is an organizer or coordinator of economic resources
- is a robust figure
- creates new combinations and disturbs previous equilibrium states
- has high need achievement
- is a "gap-filler" at the interface of different sectors[6]
- is competitive and speculative
- perceives new opportunities that others have overlooked
- is alert and searching, especially for opportunities to aggrandize[7]

Several writers have commented on the entrepreneur's need to recognize and to adapt to the prevailing culture. The concept has been applied in such varied settings as Western Europe, North America, Argentina,[8] Korea,[9] and Kenya.[10]

With such a range of attributes and synonyms, it is hardly surprising that the definition of the entrepreneur has given rise to fine hairsplitting on the one hand,[11] and to the most casual use on the other hand for successful leaders in business or other endeavors.

Numerous scholars employ components of the entrepreneurial phenomenon but use labels that are appropriate to the component that interests them. Although such an approach maximizes precision, it loses the opportunity presented by a more general concept to link behaviors that share common traits. In writing about innovative activities of German local authorities, for example, Manfred Konukiewitz and Hellmut Wollman use the label "active implementation."[12] The aspiration in this chapter is to sharpen the concept of public sector entrepreneur, and apply it to Israel.

Can There Be Entrepreneurs in the Public Sector?

The *entrepreneur* concept has been specified as appropriate *only* to profit-making private business. Entrepreneurs are said to be "proprietors";[13] people "who know how to turn a fast buck";[14] or "explorers of novel ventures (that hold) promise of large returns. . . . Rarely does this individual reside in the large bureaucratic organization."[15] "Under government direction, it is not at all clear what substitutes for the profit incentive are available. . . ."[16]

Some political scientists[17] and economists[18] have adapted the concept of entrepreneurialism to the public sector. The most complete adaptations have been made to the public-enterprise sectors of developing countries. In public enterprises there is a limited departure from the business origins of the concept. And it is generally the case in developing countries that the public sector surpasses the private sector in offering opportunities for capital accumulation and personal advancement.

It is said that entrepreneurs in the public sector

- invest their personal reputations and their careers (instead of their own money)
- aspire to programmatic success, personal notice, prestige, and/or rapid promotion (instead of financial profit)
- are most likely to appear in nonroutine positions, where they can promote change
- are likely to concentrate on one program or project in order to maximize the chances of program success, and being identified with that success in the eyes of superiors or the public
- must know how to recruit resources that are controlled by a variety of political and bureaucratic actors
- benefit from knowledge of institutional traits and the personnel of other public organizations, as well as nongovernmental groups and the mass media
- are likely to work in both formal and informal networks, cajoling, exploiting patron-client relationships, and bargaining with benefits that can be offered for benefits that can be received

The overwhelming tenor of the writing about entrepreneurialism is positive. In both the public and private sectors, however, entrepreneurial behavior can be problematic. Entrepreneurs offer the benefits of initiative and innovation but also threaten the status quo. They may redistribute money and other resources, and surpass the bounds of what is considered to be acceptable policy or procedure. They may operate in the realm of the *extralegal* or the *illegal*. There may be only a thin line between an entrepreneur and a thief or a rebel.

The Public Sector Entrepreneur Reformulated

It is appropriate both to narrow and to broaden the concept of the entrepreneur in the public sector. Without more precise specifications than appear in the list above, it hardly seems possible to distinguish entrepreneurs from successful leaders or managers. The concept of the entrepreneur seems worthy of something closer to its original usage in Schumpeter: someone whose actions are responsible for *reforming* or *revolutionizing* patterns of activity. It is this capacity to depart from the routine that may allow public sector entrepreneurs to find a way through the kinds of conundrums described in the previous chapter. It is also appropriate to broaden the application of the entrepreneurial concept beyond its appearance in the enterprise sectors that are owned by governments. Professional civil servants, political appointees, and elected political leaders are also capable of perceiving and exploiting opportunities to bring about major change.

The defining components of the public sector entrepreneur, as reformulated, are the following:

Creativity

By this is meant a capacity to exploit opportunities to create products, services, or arrangements that differ in significant ways from those that are accepted as normal or routine. The applications of the creativity can be diverse, as suggested by the numerous interpretations and reformulations of Schumpeter: techniques of financing, staffing, or organizing; the character of services that are provided, or the manner of providing existing services. Instead of the concern of some business entrepreneurs with marketing products, entrepreneurs in the public sector (who might include politicians) may create new techniques for marketing candidates, policy proposals, or the programmatic offerings of government departments.

Pursuit of aggrandizement

Financial profit figures prominently in the discussions of entrepreneurialism in the private sector. This goal is not unknown in the public sector, especially in the greatly expanded field of public enterprise.[19] However, it is best to employ a more inclusive concept in dealing with the public sector. *Aggrandizement* is parallel to, and inclusive of *financial profit*. Its definition focuses on *augmentation* and *increase*, and includes to *make greater, more powerful, richer, more exalted*.[20] The phenomena that are aggrandized may be financial resources (e.g. budget share) or control over the range of organizational, personnel, and policy issues that interest political actors.

The advantage of this short list is that it focuses on what seems to be essential in the development of the entrepreneurial concept from Schumpeter onward, at the same time that it is sufficiently broad to allow manifestations from different settings.

Israel's Environment for Entrepreneurial Behavior

Israel provides an interesting setting for public-sector entrepreneurialism. Jewish propensities to entrepreneurial behavior have been noted in both popular and serious writing.[21] The Jews of Israel are a large majority in their own country; therefore, they may not exhibit the traits that have been linked to the status of Jews as a marginal minority. Yet, most Israelis are only a generation or two removed from a marginal existence in the Diaspora. Moreover, Israel as a whole is a marginal country. Its having to struggle against both economic and military adversity may encourage the behaviors observed elsewhere among Jews who are marginal as individuals.

Several features of Israel seem likely to encourage entrepreneurial behavior in the public-sector. The small size of the society (4 million) and the personal contacts among elites in school, the military, or work facilitate the sharing of information that allows potential entrepreneurs to assess the prospects and risks of new ventures.[22]

The great size of the public-sector—relative to the economy as a whole—provides substantial resources and career prospects to those who can succeed. As noted in chapter 3, Israel's government budget ranged between 80 and 85 percent of GNP during 1978-82. The expenditures of local authorities and quasi-governmental bodies bring the total of governmental and quasi-governmental finances above 100 percent of GNP. Other large organizations operate within the framework of the Labour Federation (Histadrut) and international Jewish organizations, and deserve to be labeled "nongovernmental public-sector."

Israel has a mixed economy, which combines free enterprise along with its huge public-sector. Although the charitable and humanitarian features of Judaism contribute to Israel's substantial socialist component, the business entrepreneurial traditions of Jewish culture allow opportunities for profit-seeking business.[23] Even the commercial firms of the Labour Federation—the nucleus of Israeli socialism—recruit their young executives from the flourishing business schools of Israel, and are said to pursue profit no less than private firms. The profits of Labour Federation firms are allocated according to policies defined by the parent organization, and the company managers who accumulate the profits are targeted for career advancement.[24]

To the benefit of the public-sector entrepreneur, the organizations of the government, the Labour Federation, and international Jewry are not monolithic in their structures or procedures. They are controlled by individuals of different political parties and policy commitments, and provide opportunities for shopping around for good prospects of capital recruitment and career prospects.[25]

The culture that prevails in Israeli public-sectors respects improvisation, and permits bending the formal rules to accomplish one's ends. A comment heard from several sources helps to describe this trait. When asked about their conception of law, and how law may limit them in the performance of their jobs, a number of Israeli managers responded with the sentiment that *they would do anything not explicitly forbidden by the law.* Moreover, some indicated that when the law seemed to deter activities they considered desirable,they would seek interpretations of the law or their activities that would permit a way around the prohibitions. These views contrast with parallel expressions in nonentrepreneurial settings, where managers responded that *they can do only that which is explicitly permitted by the law.*[26] Chapter 11 deals with the pluses and minuses associated with informal behavior in the Israeli government.

Israel's economic situation may also work in behalf of entrepreneurial behavior. The economy is marked by chronic shortages of resources, in the presence of seemingly limitless demands for social services and military defense. While resource shortages by themselves might restrict entrepreneurialism, the combination of low resources and high service demands creates an environment that rewards the policymaker who can compete successfully for resources.

High inflation is said to work against entrepreneurialism by creating uncertainty;[27] however, even the triple-digit inflation that prevailed in Israel during 1980-85 may have added its own stimulus to entrepreneurial behavior. Certain Israeli managers responded to the uncertainty of inflation by creative and competitive behaviors designed to protect and enlarge the share of resources destined for their organizations.[28]

Entrepreneurial Behavior in Israel's Public Sector

The purpose of this section is to *illustrate* the existence of entrepreneurs in the public sector of Israel, chosen according to the definitional traits of creativity and aggrandizement, and to show their presence outside the limited field of public enterprises. It reports examples from among elected politicians, political appointees, and professional civil servants, who work in government departments and local authorities, as well as in public enterprises. The chapter stops short of measuring quantities of entrepreneurial manifestations, or of using the concept to define either a dependent or independent variable for purposes of systematic analysis. However, it risks some speculative conclusions about the contribution of public sector entrepreneurialism to both the strengths and the weaknesses of Israel's economic performance.

Public Enterprise

Some entrepreneurs appear in the public enterprises of Israel. Government companies in the defense sector have changed Israel from a country almost totally dependent on the willingness of others to sell it arms into a major exporter of military hardware.[29] Certain of these developments have depended on the ability of entrepreneurs to recruit capital and technology overseas. Some have done this with conventional offers of good prospects for investment. Some have made appeals that resemble those of religious bodies seeking donations for the Holy Land. The head of Israel Aircrafts

Industry, for example, has worked along with the prime minister and the minister of defense to obtain capital and technology from the United States government and U.S. defense industries for the research and development of a major combat plane.

Numerous companies of the government and the Labour Federation have recruited managers who first proved their capacity for innovation, improvisation, or leadership in the Israeli military, and who retired from duty in their forties and fifties.

There have also been entrepreneurial cases of product development and market penetration in Israel's consumer-oriented public enterprises. One newspaper story noted that a shipload of unmarked oranges had sailed from Haifa, seemingly to the markets of an unfriendly country. "Marked" oranges typically carry a distinctive Israeli brand name that would bar their entry to hostile countries. The Government Company for Coins and Medals has earned substantial profits in foreign currency by creating limited edition commemorative issues in gold, silver, and bronze on religious and patriotic themes.

Israeli public-sector entrepreneurs have been creative in building organizations. What they aggrandize by this is freedom to operate more or less as they wish. Firms owned by the government have formed subsidiaries, called "daughter companies," which in turn create their own subsidiaries, called "granddaughter companies." Such subsidiaries create numerous joint ventures, often spun off as separate companies, involving firms owned by the government, the Labour Federation, the Jewish Agency, municipalities, and universities, with the participation of private investors from Israel and/or overseas. Government authorities charged with overseeing the commercial activities of the government—like the State Comptroller and the Authority for Government Companies—do not have sufficient resources to inspect, or even enumerate all of the government's holdings. Entrepreneurs who build these complex structures benefit from access to capital by virtue of their linkages with government companies (i.e. their parent, grandparent, or greatgrandparent companies). Because the subsidiaries are not clearly definable as government companies, they avoid the procedures that have been designed to expose or to constrict the activities of government companies.[30]

One tangle of ownership appears in the diagram of a government company along with one cluster of its subsidiaries. Figure 9-1 focuses on the Dead Sea Works, a subsidiary of Israel Chemicals, and various second-, third-, and higher-generation subsidiaries and joint ventures that come under the direct or indirect control of the Dead Sea Works.

Brom Compounds illustrates the complex mixture of subsidiaries and joint ventures. It is both a daughter company of Dead Sea Works (and

Figure 9-1
A Tangle of Quasi-Governmental Organizations

```
                              ----------------
                              !Govt of Israel!
                              ----------------
-------------------           ! !    \(73%)        ----------------
!Labour Federation!           ! !     \            !Jewish Agency!
-------------------           ! !(100%) \          ----------------
      \ /                      \ /       \              \ /(16%)
-------------------    ------------------  \      -----------------
!Workers Companies!    !Israel Chemicals!   \     !National Water!
-------------------    ------------------    \    !Company       !
      \ /                      ! !            \   -----------------
-------------------           ! !(100%)       \
!Koor Industries  !            \ /                    ! !
-------------------    ------------------            ! !
      \ /              !Dead Sea Works  !            ! !
-------------------    ------------------            ! !
!Koor Chemicals   !    ! !    ! !    ! !             ! !
-------------------    ! !    ! !    ! !             ! !
      \ /              ! !    ! !    ! !             ! !
-------------------    ! !    ! !    ! !             ! !
!Negev Metals     !    ! !    ! !    ! !             ! !
-------------------    ! !    ! !    ! !             ! !
      \ /(25%)         ! !    ! !    \ /             ! !
---------------- 25%)  ! !    ! !    --------        ! !
!Brom Compounds!<------! !    ! !    !Tamhit!<-------! !
----------------       ! !    --------
      / \              \ /
      ! !   (50%)      ------------------
      ! !<-------------!Dead Sea Bromide!
                       ------------------
              \ /       ! !
          ----------    ! !
          !Eurobrom!    ! !
          ----------    \ /
              \ /       --------------------
-------------------     !Potash & Chemicals !
!Brom Netherlands!      !United Kingdom     !
-------------------     --------------------
```

Source: Ira Sharkansky *Wither the State? Politics and Public Enterprise in Three Countries* (Chatham, N.J.: Chatham House, 1979), p. 80.

therefore a granddaughter of Israel Chemicals) for 25 percent of its control, and a granddaughter of Dead Sea Works (via Dead Sea Bromide) for another 50 percent of its control, as well as being a greatgranddaughter of the Labour Federation's Koor Industries (via Koor Chemicals and Negev Metals) for another 25 percent of its control.

Local Authorities

Israel's local authorities provide another arena for the observation of entrepreneurial behavior. The formal structure subordinates these authorities to the Finance and Interior ministries, which control resources and provide programmatic oversight. The reality is something else. Chapter 5 reports how the mayors of Jerusalem, Tel Aviv, and a number of small, poor, "development towns" have learned to enhance their communities' resource allocations by behaviors that are creative and aggrandizing (i.e. entrepreneurial).

Ministerial Personnel

Senior bureaucrats and budget officers of Israeli government ministries exhibited entrepreneurial behavior in protecting their organizations from the triple-digit inflation that began in 1980.[31]

- They learned to spend their budget allotments as fast as possible, in order to realize as much value as possible from each shekel of outlay.
- They learned to delay reporting to the Finance Ministry income obtained from fees and service charges, in order that the income would be recorded against their budget accounts at the lower real value on the date reported as opposed to the date that the money was received from the public (and spent by the organization that received it).
- They learned to use the fog of inflation to hide new program ventures. They claimed more cost increases than really occurred, for example, and used the extra income to begin projects that could not receive designated funding from the Finance Ministry.

Operation Moses: The Pluses and Minuses of Entrepreneurialism

Efforts to bring Ethiopia's Jews out of that drought-ravished country revealed two sides of Israeli entrepreneurialism. The project required creativity of will, planning, and execution. While other Western countries sent food and money, Israelis undertook a project to transfer the ancient Jewish community to Israel. With an eye to an earlier movement of Jews out of Africa, the project was labeled "Operation Moses." The actual transfer of several thousand people required systematic contacts with the migrants themselves, most of whom originated in isolated villages, and arrangements with two governments that were outwardly hostile to Israel. The revolutionary Marxist regime in Ethiopia was sensitive to its citizens' wanting to flee their homeland, and the Arab regime in Sudan, where many of the Jews sought refuge from drought, was constrained from any overt contact with Israel. Over the course of several years, some 12,000 Ethiopian Jews made it through these problems, some 7,000 of them in the period of severe famine that prevailed during 1984. The movement was not a secret (it is impossible to hide 12,000 black Africans in what had been the virtually all-white Israeli society). However, it was sufficiently quiet to avoid offense to the Sudanese and Ethiopian governments. Media in Israel and overseas cooperated with efforts to avoid publicity.

Another entrepreneurial concern for financial aggrandizement brought the immigration of Ethiopians to an end. The estimated cost of $25,000 per person for migration and settlement was staggering in the midst of Israel's 1984 economic problems. Moreover, there was a well-established network of overseas donors who would respond enthusiastically to the dramatic story of the migration. There were "closed" meetings with leading fund-raisers, and letters went out to individual donors. First one and then other newspapers and television networks broke their self-imposed silence. After a week's crescendo of media attention in January 1985, the governments of both Sudan and Ethiopia proclaimed that they were innocent in the presence of crafty Zionists, and promised to halt any further movement of Jews.

At about this time incipient entrepreneurs among the Ethiopian immigrants already in Israel proved that they had learned the political game in their new country. They organized demonstrations to claim that the authorities had deliberately torpedoed the further migration of Ethiopian Jews, and they sought to mobilize public support in behalf of their community. In response to all of this officials tried to quiet the uproar, perhaps to save the reputations of the figures involved in the affair, and/or to get on with Operation Moses at a lower profile.

Limits on Israel's Public-Sector Entrepreneurs

What keeps the entrepreneurs of Israel's public sector from running amuck, and creating a chaos of unrestrained demands on the country's resources? One constraint may lie in the number of entrepreneurs who actually exist. The material above demonstrates that *entrepreneurialism exists* in Israel's public sector; it does not indicate the *incidence* of entrepreneurialism among Israel's public servants.(The literature on entrepreneurialism in the private sector is also lacking in quantitative indicators for entrepreneurial behavior.) Many of Israel's public-sector managers do not behave as entrepreneurs. Like the stereotyped bureaucrat, they seem content to do their jobs routinely, without taking risks.

The formal structure of Israel's government provides some constraints against excessive entrepreneurialism. The Finance Ministry is the principal source of oversight and control. Its separate units include the Budget Department (concerned with preparing budget proposals for the cabinet's consideration), the Accountant General (concerned with making periodic financial allotments to governmental bodies from their budget allocations), the Civil Service Commission (concerned with the number and remuneration of personnel in government ministries, local authorities, and government companies), and the Authority for Government Companies (concerned with overseeing the procedures and financial reports of government companies).

The existence of entrepreneurs in organizations charged with the supervision and control of line units also minimizes the damage that could be done by unrestrained entrepreneurs. Individuals with control responsibilities manifest entrepreneurial behavior by creative efforts to aggrandize with respect to the goals of their organizations. In these cases, aggrandizement entails *increasing* the resources under the effective control of the supervisory units, via *limiting* the resources that flow to other units.

During the era of high inflation, personnel in the Finance Ministry introduced a number of innovative procedures to counter the tactics of spending ministries. The aggregate of these procedures pressured the spending ministries to provide greater justifications for the resources they demanded.

- The Finance Ministry began each budget cycle with an artificially low estimate of the inflation expected in the coming fiscal year, and provided budgetary adjustments according to that low forecast.
- The Finance Ministry upgraded its midyear allotment procedures. Instead of sending to the ministries one-fourth of each annual budget more or less automatically every three months, the Finance Ministry created a monthly allotment exercise that required justifications for each allotment.

As a result of these moves, spending ministries began each fiscal year in the hole, with fewer resources than actually needed to keep up with inflation. Not only did they have to justify supplementary budgets in the midst of the year but each month they had to justify the already-budgeted amounts that they stood to be allotted during the coming month.

Israel's control officers have proved willing to discipline public-sector entrepreneurs who go beyond the boundaries of acceptable behavior. The

Finance Ministry employed the dynamics of inflation against those thought to be working against the ministry's policies. By delaying a payment to a body thought to be breaking its rules, the Finance Ministry penalized the errant body by a reduction in the real value of the money received.

Tel Aviv's mayor did not escape without cost from his entrepreneurial tactic of going into unauthorized debt, and then waiting for the Finance Ministry to pay his bills, as described in chapter 5. As its price for one bailout of the municipality, the Finance Ministry insisted that the municipality reduce its work force by 1,000 positions, or some 10 percent of its establishment.

The State Comptroller—responsible to the Israeli parliament (Knesset)—has uncovered several excesses of entrepreneurial behavior that have led to action by other bodies with disciplinary powers. Chapter 11 will return to the role of the State Comptroller in limiting excessive behaviors in Israel's public-sector.

Some entrepreneurs have found themselves accused of criminal offenses. The head of the Labour Federation's Sick Fund solicited funds for his political party from contractors who wanted to do business with the Sick Fund. If that showed entrepreneurialism, it also broke the rules of rational, neutral bureaucracy. The person was charged, found guilty, and spent several years in prison.

Control officers also mete out embarrassment to those who break their rules. During the first weeks of the war in Lebanon, hospitals that treated the wounded sought special grants to cover their costs. The budget office of the Health Ministry found one hospital requesting money to replace 100 dozen fever thermometers. The budget office was sure that it caught an aspiring entrepreneur in a gross exaggeration. It distributed the story through the country's bureaucratic grapevine, informed the mass media, and held up substantial payments to the hospital as a sign of the ministry's disapproval.

Widely shared values may also constrain the behavior of public-sector entrepreneurs. The elite of various sectors recognize that resources are limited, and sense that they should not seek too much for their own programs. Research among the kibbutzim of Israel indicates that "team entrepreneurialism" is facilitated by intimacy and mutual trust.[32] Survey research finds that Israelis are well informed about public affairs, and are willing to make personal sacrifices for the general good.[33] *Look after yourself* is a legitimate value in Israel, with deep roots in Jewish thought. At the same time, *Don't be a pig* is also an important value. The Hebrew sage Hillel put it this way two millenia ago: "Who am I if I am not for myself? Who am I if I think only about myself?"

A Speculative Discussion: Implications of Public-Sector Entrepreneurialism for the Strengths and Weaknesses of Israel's Economy

How can the existence of entrepreneurialism in Israel's public-sector be squared with the numerous signs of difficulty in the country's economy? As noted in earlier chapters, inflation ranged above 100 percent annually during 1980-85. The economy's growth has stagnated since 1973. Foreign debt has grown, and reserves of foreign currency have shrunk to the point where the government has sought emergency assistance.

One assessment of these events points to the entrepreneurialism in Israel's public-sector! The traits of creativity and aggrandizement help to explain both the earlier impressive growth and the problems that have occurred since 1973. There was too much entrepreneurialism in the wrong places. Entrepreneurialism among officials concerned to finance their activities was more prominent than entrepreneurialism among officers concerned to limit government outlays.

How much of Israel's public-sector entrepreneurialism reflects Jewish cultural heritage? and What is the future of public-sector entrepreneurialism in the modern state where Jews are the majority? These, too, are questions that invite speculation. Entrepreneurialism seems to be rooted in the national culture. There is a liveliness that reminds one of an economist's effort to define the entrepreneur "as active, creative, and human."[34] The fervor with which politicians and opinion leaders demand resources for education, the arts, social services, and the military reflects a political economy that relegates economizing to secondary importance.

Notes

1. Yehezkel Dror, *Public Policymaking Reexamined* (San Francisco: Chandler, 1968), pp. 149-53.
2. William Glade, "The Levantines in Latin America," *American Economic Review: Papers and Proceedings* 73 (May 1983): 118-22.
3. Peter Kilby, "An Entrepreneurial Problem" *American Economic Review: Papers and Proceedings* 73 (May 1983): 107-11.
4. Third edition (New York: Harper, 1950), p. 132.
5. Paul H. Wilken, *Entrepreneurship: A Comparative and Historical Study* (Norwood, N.J.: Ablex, 1979); Robert F. Hebert and Albert N. Link, *The Entrepreneur* (New York: Praeger, 1982).
6. Harvey Leibenstein, "Entrepreneurship and Development," *American Economic Review: Papers and Proceedings* 58 (May 1968): 60-63.
7. Israel M. Kirzner, *Competition and Entrepreneurship* (Chicago: University of Chicago Press, 1973).

8. Thomas C. Cochran and Ruben E. Reina, *Entrepreneurship in Argentine Culture: Torcuato di Tella and S.I.A.M.* (Philadelphia: University of Pennsylvania Press, 1962).

9. Leroy P. Jones and Il Sakong *Government, Business, and Entrepreneurship in Economic Development: The Korean Case* (Cambridge: Harvard University Press, 1980).

10. Peter Marris and Anthony Somerset, *African Businessman: A Study of Entrepreneurship and Development in Kenya* (London: Routledge & Kegan Paul, 1971).

11. Kirzner, *Competition and Entrepreneurship*, p. 31.

12. "Urban Innovation: A Response to Deficiencies of the Intervention and Welfare State?" *Research in Urban Policy* 5, no. 1 (1985): 327-39.

13. Richard Scase and Robert Goffee, *The Entrepreneurial Middle Class* (London: Croom Helm, 1982).

14. Mark Carson, *The Entrepreneur: An Economic Theory*, Totowa N.J.: Barnes & Noble, 1982).

15. Joshua Ronen, ed., *Entrepreneurship* (Lexington, Mass.: Lexington Books, 1983), p. 1.

16. Kirzner, *Competition and Entrepreneurship*, p. 230.

17. For example, Dennis L. Dresang, "Public Sector Entrepreneurialism," *Administrative Science Quarterly* 18 (March 1973): 76-85.

18. For example, William P. Glade, "Entrepreneurship in the State Sector: CONASUPO of Mexico," in *Entrepreneurs in Cultural Context*, ed. Sidney M. Greenfield et al (Albuquerque: University of New Mexico Press, 1979), pp. 191-224.

19. See, for example, Raymond Vernon, ed., *Big Business and the State: Changing Relations in Western Europe* (Cambridge: Harvard University Press, 1974).

20. *Webster's New World Dictionary of the American Language* (Cleveland: World Publishing Company, 1974).

21. David McClelland, *The Achieving Society* (New York: Van Nostrand, 1961).

22. On the importance of information for entrepreneurs, see Ronen. *Entrepreneurship.*

23. On government-owned firms, see Yair Aharoni, *State-Owned Enterprises in Israel and Abroad* (Tel-Aviv: Goma, 1979)(Hebrew).

24. Haim Barkai, "Theory and Praxis of the Histadrut Industrial Sector," *Jerusalem Quarterly* 26 (Winter 1982): 96-108; Michael Shalev, "Labor, State and Crisis: An Israeli Case Study," *Industrial Relations* 23 (Fall 1984): 362-86.

25. Gerald E. Caiden, *Israel's Administrative Culture* (Berkeley: University of California, Institute of Government Studies, 1970).

26. Ira Sharkansky, *Wither the State: Politics and Public Enterprise in Three Countries,*(Chatham, N.J.:Chatham House, 1979).

27. Michael J. Boskin, "The Fiscal Environment for Entrepreneurship," in *The Environment for Entrepreneurship*, ed. Calvin A. Kent (Lexington, Mass.: Lexington Books, 1984), pp. 59-68.

28. Ira Sharkansky, *What Makes Israel Tick? How Domestic Policymakers Cope with Constraints* (Chicago: Nelson-Hall, 1985), ch. 5.

29. Alex Mintz, "An Empirical Study of Military-Industrial Linkages in Israel," *Armed Forces and Society* (forthcoming).

30. Sharkansky, *Wither the State?*

31. Sharkansky, *What Makes Israel Tick?* ch. 5.

32. William J. Baumol, "Toward Operational Modes of Entrepreneurship," in *Entrepreneurship* ed. Joshua Ronen (Lexington, Mass.: Lexington Books, 1983), pp. 29-48.
33. Russel A. Stone, *Social Change in Israel: Attitudes and Events, 1967-79*, (New York: Praeger, 1982).
34. Kirzner, *Competition and Entrepreneurship*, p. 35.

10

Policy-Making by Indirection

- During much of the period marked by high inflation, it was difficult for the Israeli government to combat inflation by cutting in a significant way the budgets of government ministries. The ministers were not willing to offer their programs for major cuts and thus risk the loss of personal status in a competitive political game, but the government could reduce the real value of the government budget by not increasing wages and other outlays at the same rate as the ongoing inflation.
- The salaries of most Israeli wage earners are defined in formal agreements involving the Labour Federation (Histadrut), the government, and representatives of the country's large employers. It is difficult to increase the salary paid to members of one occupation without provoking demands from other occupations who find that their place in the economic pecking order has been upset. However, it is possible to award a fringe benefit that is said, tongue in cheek, to apply to the special working conditions of the occupation.
- Reducing Israel's inflation was announced as a prime target by each of the five finance ministers from 1977. Most of the time, the principal strategy was one of chipping away via one or another of the variables that were said to hold the key to the inflation. When the annual rate of inflation calculated on a monthly basis approached 1,000 in late 1984, major actors in the government, Labour Federation, and the private sector conceded that they had lost control of the economy. Although they still could not agree on fundamental reforms, they did agree on wage and price controls for a three month period. The announced goal was to calm the economy, stop inflation, and provide a period for the policymakers to reach agreement on more fundamental reforms.

The above examples illustrate policy-making by indirection.[1] What officials cannot achieve directly, they may be able to achieve indirectly. If they cannot pursue A, they might pursue B in the hope that it will lead to something that approximates A. If an element of a conundrum is a fixed blockage in the way of certain solutions, indirection may be an appropriate coping strategy.

The kinds of problems that can frustrate the achievement of primary goals are well documented.[2] There may be opposition in the arenas where policymakers must achieve agreement about goals or means. Policy advocates may not have access to sufficient resources. Domestic interests or foreign governments may seek to upset planning or implementation. Opposition may develop among one's own administrators who must cooperate for effective implementation.[3] Clients may not be inclined to accept the program that is offered to them. Opinion leaders may find that the policy threatens important values.

Policymakers have devised a number of ways to cope with economic, political, or cultural limitations. They include compromise, bargaining, persuasion, and incrementalism. Elements of indirection are present in each of these other techniques, and indirection is also a distinguishable technique in its own right. Indirection appears in these other techniques insofar as each of them pursues something other than of a policymaker's own primary goal. Compromise and bargaining are ways of defining goals that are acceptable to various participants in a policy-making arena. Persuasion is a device for convincing protagonists to give up their primary goals for something that is close to or similar to one's own primary goals. Incrementalism is a way of achieving goals in stages, which might be defined as the pursuit of primary goals indirectly via intermediate stages. Compromise, bargaining, persuasion, incrementalism—and indirection— are devices for *satisficing*,[4] i.e. achieving something that is acceptable, even if it is less than one's full desires.

In international relations and military planning, indirection is a classic device to mislead one's enemies. In domestic politics it may also be useful to pursue objectives in stages or indirectly. Domestic policymakers sometimes conceal their intentions, or even seek to mislead their opponents.

Indirection is not a monopoly of policymakers. It also appears in commerce, medicine, agriculture, and design. When a shop offers a bargain, it is engaging in indirection: it seeks to increase income (A) by reducing its profit—or even taking a loss—on certain items (B). It may reach A by a "loss leader" that attracts lots of shoppers to buy the items that are reduced in price, and attracts some of them to buy other items once they are in the store. Indirection appears in medicine as part of the treatment for patients with irreparable kidneys or hearts. To permit the patient's body to accept a transplanted organ, physicians use drugs that will attack the body's defense mechanism against foreign objects. Thus to deal with the organ (A), it is necessary to weaken the body's defense mechanism (B). Indirection appears in agriculture when farmers sow one crop that puts nitrogen into the soil so as to increase the yield of another crop in the next season. Indirection appears in design via the tricks that attract the eye to see things that are not there, like motion, distance, or depth.

Clarifying Policy-Making by Indirection

Indirection appears to be subsumed in many of the devices that policymakers use to cope with their adversities. The problem with such a concept is that it risks becoming a synonym for political savvy. The challenge of defining indirection in policy-making is to produce a formulation that captures its breadth while providing sufficient precision to justify its treatment as a distinct phenomenon.

Dictionary definitions of *indirection* hint at the content of the political concept. *Indirection* is defined as *deviating*; *roundabout*; *not straight at the person or thing aimed at.* Normative elements appear in secondary meanings like *not straightforward*; *not fair and open*; and *dishonest.*[5]

Indirection occurs when policymakers pursue *something else instead of their primary goal.* It involves departing from one's original goal (A) in order to achieve something that is close to it via a B. The B may be an intermediate step on the way to A, or a different formulation that will avoid some of the opposition that had been expressed to A.

This chapter fleshes out the concept of policy-making by indirection by exploring three cases of Israeli economic policy-making. The description of each case will specify the primary goal; the barriers to the simple achievement of the primary goal; and the form of indirection that is pursued; and will offer a summary assessment of success or failure in achieving something close to the primary goal.

Budget Cutting by Erosion

Israel's economic situation seemed to require cuts in the government's budget. Among academics there may be some dispute as to whether budget deficits cause inflation or inflation causes budget deficits;[6] however, each Israeli finance minister since 1977 has called for real cuts in government outlays.

The description of the blockages to overt budget cutting, and the explanation of the indirect budget cutting pursued by Israeli finance ministers begins with the political pride and competitiveness of ministers and their parties. Israeli governments are coalitions of political parties, none of which has ever won a majority in the Knesset. Each minister is both a leading member of a party and a representative of that party in the government. The parties have agreed to form a government together, but there remains competition between them. None wants to approach the next election with the reputation of having done less well than other parties in the coalition. There is also competition among the ministers as individuals. They are likely to be seeking ever-higher places in their parties and in the government, or at least are likely to be concerned to maintain their current places. For these reasons, it is difficult for any minister to accept an overt budget cut.

How to achieve what cannot be done directly? The Finance Ministry generally failed to realize overt cuts in the budget (A). In response, it worked indirectly to allow inflation to limit the real size of each ministry's budget (B). Before the start of each fiscal year the Finance Ministry began the budget process with a projection of inflation that was artificially low. The purpose of the low projection was to justify budget increases that will be insufficient for each ministry to maintain its current level of services, and would force it to justify supplementary allocations during the fiscal year.

The Finance Ministry also changed its allotment procedures from more-or-less routine allotments of one-fourth each ministry's annual budget every three months to a monthly procedure that required detailed justifications for each allotment. Together with the artificially low projection of coming inflation, monthly allotments pressured ministries into justifying their budget outlays, and—it was hoped—keeping actual outlays below the rate of inflation. If the indirection succeeded, it would reduce the overall government budget in real terms (i.e. after controlling for inflation). Although no minister would have to admit an overt budget cut to political competitors, the budgets should go down in real terms, with salutary consequences for inflation, government debt, and other aspects of economic well-being.

A look backward over the course of seven fiscal years shows some signs of success in this policy-making by indirection, and other signs of abject failure.[7] As reported in chapter 6, only five of 36 major budget categories had larger outlays in 1984 than 1978, after correcting for inflation. If the budget for debt service is removed, then the entire budget was 16 percent lower (in real terms) in 1984 than in 1978. In the same period of time, however, the total budget (including debt service) increased by some 26 percent in real terms.

For the period 1980-82, it seemed that the government might be holding inflation in the range of 100-130 percent. However, annual rates reached above 200 percent in 1983, and near 400 percent for 1984. There were also other signs of serious economic problems. GNP per capita, controlling for inflation, increased over the 1978-84 period by only 1.3 percent per year; the country's foreign debt fluctuated around 125 per cent of current GNP throughout the period; and foreign-currency reserves declined from 53 to 45 percent of current GNP. In 1984 the government sought emergency economic aid from the United States in addition to the $3 billion annual aid already committed.

The Finance Ministry's avoidance of overt budget cuts did not persuade ministers to accept budget erosions in real terms. They did not believe that they would be treated equally if they remained passive. There was unremitting competitive game-playing between spending ministries intent on gaining a bit more in allocations and the Finance Ministry intent on minimizing their allocations. This gaming consumed time and energies that might have been used to improve the implementation of existing programs, or to develop innovations.

Stopping Inflation for the Time Being

In the autumn of 1984 it became increasing clear that the preferred strategy of nibbling away at the causes of Israeli inflation had not succeeded. The situation was like that of an obese person who had tried to lose weight gradually but had not stopped eating favorite foods. The monthly price increases published in October were extrapolated to an annual inflation near 1,000 percent.

The government's response to the threatening prospect of 1,000 percent inflation was to negotiate a three-month "package deal" of wage and price controls with the Labour Federation and Industrialists' Association. The announced goal was to achieve a calming of consumers, wage earners and business firms, and a period in which to seek a more thoroughgoing reform of the economy. This package constituted the B, or an intermediate goal, pursued in the hope that it would help in the primary goal (A) of dealing with the country's chronic inflation.

The agreement of the Labour Federation and the Industrialists' Association to the package deal was achieved in part by the government's willingness to continue sizable subsidies of public transportation, basic foods, and exports. These were funded by domestic and foreign borrowing. The monthly rate of inflation dropped from 24.3 percent to 3.7 percent. Although the consumer price index could come down in the short run, the policy could not continue without eventual crises of foreign currency reserves and intolerable budget outlays for debt repayment. Indeed, after two months of price increases in the modest ranges of 3 to 5 percent, the monthly consumer price index increased to 19.3 percent for March 1985.

Income Increases via Fringe Benefits

Israel's highly centralized economy provides a major barrier to increasing the salaries of wage earners. Each occupational group is organized, and has bargained its way to a place on the national salary scale. As a result, a change in one group's salary will generate demands from occupations higher and lower on the scale that their salaries be increased in proportion.

When the overt increase in a group's salary (A) is blocked, it may be possible to pursue an increase in incomes indirectly. The B is the award of fringe benefits that are said to apply to the special working conditions of a single occupation. The hope is that other occupations will accept this special deal, or at least be delayed in pursuing their own special claims.

It makes some sense for electric company linemen to receive a "height allowance," inasmuch as they do work high up on utility poles. It is less clear why university teachers should receive an allowance for being "on call" after hours (which they won after similar awards were given to military officers, and then physicians and nurses), why laboratory technicians should receive an "effort" allowance, or why one group after another should receive—on the earlier pattern of the teachers—a grant for continued education.

This use of indirection has preserved labor peace only with respect to salary. Conflicts occur on the field of fringe benefits. At one point the "salary" of a university professor, for example, was only 31 percent of total monthly income; the rest was provided by 13 additions to the salary.

Analysis

In each of these cases, it was impractical to pursue an original goal (A). Instead, policymakers sought a B, which was either an intermediate accomplishment that might assist in the eventual achievement of A, or a reformulation of A, which would achieve the important ingredients of A.

In the cases of budget cutting by erosion and income increases via fringe benefits, the B was a reformulation of A. Instead of cutting ministerial budgets outright, the Finance Ministry sought to increase them at less than the rate of inflation, and thereby reduce them in real terms by eroding their buying power. Instead of pursuing the difficult route of increasing salaries, representatives of management and labor find reasons for paying each group of employees fringe benefits that are said to be peculiar to their occupational needs.

The case of stopping inflation for the time being via wage-price controls was a B conceived to be an intermediate stage on the way to the A of dealing systematically with the causes of inflation. This B would calm the economy, and provide time for policymakers to reach agreement on a fundamental series of reforms.

Each of these cases could be described as successes, but only superficially or in the short term. Budget cutting by erosion contributed to the stabilization of Israeli inflation in the range of 100-130 percent for a period of three years, and over the longer period of 1978-84 kept most budget items from increasing their allocations in real terms. Yet the indirection could not overcome the inflationary pressures built into the election campaigns of 1981 and 1984. The government behaved as suggested by the literature on the "political business cycle."[8] In both election campaigns the government increased subsidies, reduced taxes, or provided other economic benefits to the voters. The Lebanese war that began in 1982 provided its own contributions to heightened inflation.

Stopping inflation for the time being did produce a sharp reduction in the monthly cost-of-living index; however, it was accomplished at the price of continued subsidies, which caused problems of additional debt, and the feelings in particular sectors that the controls worked to their disadvantage. The three-month period of the controls was not long enough for the coalition government, the Labour Federation, and the Industrialists' Association to solve the economic problems that had eluded them since inflation began its increase years before. After only two months of low consumer price increases, the monthly index began to move up sharply.

In the case of increasing incomes via fringe benefits, superficial success was a poor substitute for fundamental reform. The salaries of various occupations remain more or less fixed in relation to one another, but the special fringe benefits awarded to one group cannot remain secret. One group after another receives fringe benefits similar to those granted elsewhere, generally with not even a pretense that the new fringe benefit is tailored to their occupational needs.

The limitations of policy-making by indirection described here may reflect the unrepresentative traits of these cases, or special problems in Israel's political economy. However, certain more general traits of policy-making by indirection seem likely to produce frustration. The technique seeks to evade or avoid blockages in the policy-making setting, yet the blockages may persist in the damage they can cause to efforts that are similar to those earlier deflected. The B chosen as an intermediate goal or a substitute for the original A seems likely to encounter the same or similar problems as frustrated the original A.

Even if the advantages of policy-making by indirection aid in the resolution of disputes, the quality of resolutions may be unsatisfactory. Opponents who see the achievement of something close to A via B may react with hostility in the near or distant future. They may attack B at the stage of implementation, and thereby minimize its actual contribution to the achievement of A.

It may be difficult to know what is the A and what is the B. When policymakers proceed by indirection they may intend to confuse their opponents as to their nominal and their real goals. At times they may confuse themselves, as when some members of a policy-making group (e.g. a committee of administrators or legislators) intend B as the real goal, while others in the same group see B as a route to A. The verbiage that comes along with an effort at indirect policy-making is not likely to explain motives candidly.

The political accountability of government may suffer if elected representatives and citizens cannot discern what is real and what is indirection. Legislators come to doubt the assertions of the executive branch or the leaders of their own parties in the legislature, while citizens doubt the candor of government generally.[9] When political leaders call on their colleagues and the public to make personal sacrifices for the general good, they count on a trust that may have been frittered away by previous instances of indirection. Israeli ministers were quick to perceive that the Finance Ministry was basing each year's initial budget upon projections of inflation that were lower than actually expected. What ensued was intense gaming, and not a little cynicism.

The cases considered here suggest a series of questions that can be used to evaluate the past use of policy-making by indirection or the proposal to make policy indirectly.

- Has indirection succeeded (or is it likely to succeed) in evading the original blockage(s) to A? Or has it merely postponed or shifted the encounter of these blockages to some other time or some other juncture in the processes of policy-making and implementation?
- Has indirection gained (or is it likely to gain) enough advantage to be worth its costs? These costs may be expressed as time lost in assessing and planning to deal with the problems that blocked the straightforward achievement of A; or in the confusion and resulting cynicism that may occur among policymakers and policy clients as to what is the real goal, and what is to be only an intermediate stage or a reformulation of the original goal.

The tale of the little boy who cried wolf is a story of indirection that went bad. The boy sought attention (A) by calling wolf (B). On the day that a wolf really appeared, his companions thought he was deceiving them again.

Notes

1. Thanks are due to Aaron Wildavsky for encouraging the author to develop the label and the concept.
2. A summary work in this genre is Charles Lindblom, *The Policy-Making Process* (Englewood Cliffs, N.J.: Prentice-Hall, 1979).

3. For a recent piece in this burgeoning literature, see Daniel A. Mazmanian and Paul A. Sabatier, *Implementation and Public Policy* (Glenview, Ill.: Scott, Foresman, 1983).

4. Herbert Simon, *Administrative Behavior* (New York: Free Press, 1976).

5. *Webster's New World Dictionary of the American Language* (Cleveland: World Publishing Company, 1974.)

6. George Guess and Kenneth Koford, "Inflation, Recession and the Federal Budget Deficit (or Blaming Economic Problems on a Statistical Mirage)," *Policy Sciences* 17 (December 1984): 385-402.

7. For a general survey of recent economic events in Israel see Yoram Ben-Porath, "The Economy of Israel: Maturing Through Crises" (Jerusalem: Falk Institute, 1985).

8. See Yoram Ben-Porath, "The Years of Plenty and the Years of Famine—A Political Business Cycle," *Kyklos* 28 (1975): 400-3; Michael Bruno and Stanley Fischer, "The Inflationary Process in Israel: Shocks and Accommodation" (Jerusalem: Falk Institute, 1984).

9. See N. H. Nie, S. Verba, and J. R. Petrockik, *The Changing American Voter* (Cambridge: Harvard University Press, 1976).

11

Government Corruption or Acceptable Flexibility? Sorting Out the Differences

Israel has extensive governmental controls on the one hand, and allows many informal exemptions from the controls on the other hand. An assessment of its procedures for making and implementing public policy requires sorting out numerous evasions of the laws and other formal rules by public sector bodies. Should explicit violations be labeled as corruption,[1] or as reasonable exercises of flexibility that "circumvent the snarls" of central controls?[2]

The dominance of Israel's government is described in previous chapters. It is the most economy involved government among Western democracies. The government also plays a major role in setting wages and prices, and details numerous restrictions on the procedures of organizations in the public and private sectors.

A senior official in one of the government's control bodies described the flexibility that prevails amidst numerous rules when he said that "surpassing formal limits is part of the game." Widely ackowledged violations of the formal rules include the following:

- Municipalities continue to borrow money from banks and run up sizable debts with contractors and suppliers despite regulations to the contrary that are supposed to be implemented by the Finance and Interior ministries.
- Municipalities, government companies, and other public institutions like universities and hospitals fail to transmit to the Finance Ministry according to the required schedules the income tax payments that they withhold from their employees' wages.
- Senior employees of government departments generally report that they have driven their private cars for public business more than is truly the case; they thereby transform an arrangement that is formally one of repayment for expenditures into one that is actually another addition to their monthly income.
- The country's commercial banks routinely manipulated the value of their shares in the stock exchange for more than 11 years, despite a

number of contrary rules that were to be administered by the Bank of Israel, the Finance Ministry, the Stock Exchange, and the Securities Commission. The failure of these bodies to activate their controls was explained, in part, as a way to grant the banks more freedom to attract capital and to induce savings on the part of the public. The bubble of public confidence burst in the autumn of 1983, and there began a compound scandal of finance and politics that is still an item of controversy.[3]

What Is Corruption? and What Is Acceptable Flexibility?

The selection of negative or positive labels for what occurs frequently in Israel (i.e. corruption or acceptable flexibility) depends on choices that can be made from what has been written about governmental corruption, as well on one's judgment of the behaviors at issue. The literature on corruption offers numerous definitions of that concept.[4]

One definition of *corruption* is *behavior that departs from the requirements of laws and other official rules*. Yet, many writers assert that this definition is too simple and too strict. Some distinguish corruption from activity that violates formal rules but that benefits large groups, and has the support of public opinion or conventional morality.[5] In a similar vein, others define corruption as behavior that seeks to distort the activities of public bodies in order to advance personal, or "private-regarding" interests, as opposed to public interests.[6] It is common to write about behaviors that are more or less corrupt—or about corruption that is black, gray, or white—insofar as the behavior departs *more or less* from legal or cultural norms.[7]

Comments of Israeli officials and observers reflect these positions in the literature. They also serve to distinguish, in general terms, what is acceptable in their culture as reasonable provisions for flexibility, and what is condemned as corruption. The same official who said that "surpassing formal limits is part of the game" also insisted that "surpassing informal limits is not (part of the game)." Israeli officials use fraud, bribery, and embezzlement as synonyms for corruption. Some of their colleagues have been convicted and jailed for these offenses.

Officials describe behavior that is accepted informally—although it might be technically illegal—as including that which has the tacit acceptance of other officials, which benefits public organizations or substantial constituencies, and which involves resources that are termed "moderate." Once the mass media make an issue about behaviors that are formally against the rules, however, governmental control officers say that they are constrained to follow the official rules. Observers concede that there are problems in drawing lines at each of the points between behaviors that are—and are not—acceptable.

Clarifying the Lines between Acceptable and Unacceptable Behaviors

Much of the writing about governmental corruption laments the impenetrability of the topic for systematic research. Those who engage in illegal behaviors are said to leave no tracks. This may be true generally; however, Israel presents the case of an aggressive and sophisticated State Comptroller whose *Annual Reports* and other documents can be mined systematically in order to discern which behaviors are more or less acceptable.[8]

The State Comptroller has a wide-ranging mandate to inquire into bodies of the state, plus local authorities and those organizations in which the government has a share in its management or financing. The standards of judgment available to the State Comptroller include the legal compliance of audited activities, and whether they "have operated economically, efficiently and in a morally irreproachable manner."[9] The published results of the State Comptroller's inquiries are presented to the Knesset (Israel's parliament) and available to the public. *Annual Reports* that range upward from 1,000 pages summarize each year's work.

Much of the material in the State Comptroller's reports focuses on behaviors that reflect poor judgment or incompetence. This has no relevance for issues of flexibility or corruption. However, a significant minority of the findings provide fuel for this analysis. They cite governmental organizations for breaking the formal rules, and reveal a gradation from mild to severe censure.

The State Comptroller also Breaks the Rules: The Issue of 14c

Section 14c of the State Comptroller Law seems to direct the reference of suspected criminal violations to the Government's Legal Advisor: "Where an inspection has revealed that an inspected body has operated in a manner arousing suspicion of a criminal act, the Comptroller shall bring the matter to the knowledge of the Legal Advisor to the Government." What reads on the surface as a mandate to refer suspicious operations to the government's Legal Advisor is actually interpreted as a permissive statement, including a grant of discretion to the State Comptroller as to whether particular behavior warrants designation as arousing suspicion of a criminal act. This pragmatic interpretation of Section 14c is itself an example of the informal norms that pervade Israeli government. Also, by serving to limit criminal prosecutions for illegal behavior, the pragmatic interpretation of Section 14c has become one of the points in defining what is considered corruption in the Israeli context, and what is considered the acceptable exercise of flexibility. When the state comptroller refrains from refering certain activities to the government's Legal Advisor, he signals that the activity in question is not a violation of Israel's informal rules.

The State Comptroller's reading of discretion into Section 14c requires that the staff overlook not only the mandatory language in 14c itself but also a section in the Israeli criminal code that applies the coverage of criminal law to acts of commission or omission cited in regular law when they occur in the public sector.[10]

According to personnel of the State Comptroller, strict interpretations of Section 14c would require the referral to the Legal Advisor to the Government of so many findings as to overload the Legal Advisor, and destroy morale in the public service. They cite language from the criminal code itself that would restrict its application to certain violations that could be labeled serious.[11] They indicate that cases must show clear indications of fraud, bribery, embezzlement, or personal profit to warrant referral to the Legal Advisor.

Personnel of the State Comptroller assert that their primary task is not the identification of criminal activity. The latest *Annual Report* included findings on some 250 major items—many of which included numerous components—but staff personnel indicate that they refer fewer than 10 issues per year to the Legal Advisor. For the most part, they are content to publish their findings without formal referrals. Personnel say that this satisfies the essential responsibilities of the State Comptroller, and leaves in the hands of other officials the decision to accept or restrict the practices that find their way into the State Comptroller's reports.

It is not customary for the State Comptroller to announce its referrals to the Legal Advisor of the Government. This may be due to the finding that the Legal Advisor moves only a small percentage of the referrals further to formal investigations by the police and eventual prosecutions. The Legal Advisor as well as the State Comptroller seems concerned to distinguish cases that require firm control from those that are acceptable exercises of administrative discretion, or that lack the quality of evidence to substantiate criminal proceedings.

Grading Censures from Mild to Severe

Despite the restraint of the State Comptroller with respect to calling in the Legal Advisor to the Government, its *Annual Reports* allow qualitative analysis to define what is more and less acceptable to this auditor of public activities. Each item contained in the *Annual Report* includes a highlighted summary of findings and judgments, which can be classified according to the degree of censure that it contains. Table 11-1 specifies criteria for ranking the summaries, from mild to severe censure. These criteria were derived from an initial reading of the State Comptroller's *Reports*, guided by conversations with individuals active in the audit of public bodies in Israel, including senior members of the State Comptroller's staff.

Ninety-one separate items included in the State Comptroller's *Annual Reports* for 1983 and 1984 were judged to cite audited bodies for violations of the law or other formal rules. The summary of each item was scored on a scale of 1 to 10, according to the severity of censure, as guided by the criteria listed in table 11-1. The judgments made were qualitative, guided by the criteria specified in table 11-1. Subsequently these scores were compared with the length of the total reports and the length of the summary about each item. The literature on content analysis indicates that the length of a report dedicated to an issue will, on the average, signify the degree of concern for the issue.[12]

The censures that were scored most severe (i.e. grades 8-10) indeed were attached to reports that averaged 36 percent longer and summaries that averaged 41 percent longer than censures that were scored least severe (grades 1-3). In the discussion that follows, the cases of severe censure will be compared to those of mild censure in order to define the kinds of administrative action that violate the informal as well as the formal norms of Israeli government.

Table 11-1
Elements Indicating Severity of Censure
in the Summaries of the State Comptroller

Separate judgments about the severity of censure were made with respect to the elements included within each of the three groups of criteria shown below. The items within each group are ranked according to the degree of censure that they reflect. A summary score for each case was derived by averaging the scores assigned to each of the three elements listed here.

1. Length and generality of report:
   Brief description in general terms
   Lengthy description in specific terms
2. Quality of adjectives used to describe the findings:
   "serious"
   "most serious"
   "extremely serious"
   issues that are cited as violations of "moral" or "criminal" norms
3. Recommendations:
   Call for immediate action on the part of the audited body
   Call for immediate cessation of activities found to be at fault
   Call for repayments or other reversals of activities found to be at fault
   Call for the specific involvement of other bodies to control the activities that were audited
   Call for extraordinary actions, such as formulation of policy by the government, or the convening of a national commission of inquiry

Findings: Defining the Limits of Administrative Flexibility

Israel's State Comptroller is a dynamic element in the country's system for policy-making and evaluation. Its censures of improper activity changed in the direction of increasing severity during the 1983-84 period. The later *Annual Report* was longer by 25 percent than the earlier; it contained twice as many items that cited administrative bodies for violations, and these items averaged twice as high in their scores indicating the severity of censures.

The increased assertiveness of the State Comptroller may reflect the personal influence of the state comptroller himself, or an objective worsening of governmental conditions. The *Annual Report* for 1983 was the first compiled completely during the tenure of the present comptroller, and he may still have been feeling his way. By his second year in office he was showing an expansive view of his role. He was also having problems with senior personnel who felt that he was exceeding the bounds defined for his office by tradition and good sense.

The increased severity of the State Comptroller's censures may reflect the worsening of governmental conditions from 1983 to 1984. Inflation increased from just over 200 per cent in 1983 to nearly 1,000 on an annual basis late in 1984. With this increase in inflation there were also increased pressures to reduce government outlays and increase efficiency.

To define qualitative differences between violations of the formal norms that are more or less acceptable, items in the State Comptroller's *Annual Reports* that drew the lightest censures were compared with those that drew the most severe censures. This comparison found severe censures associated with

- prima facie evidence of fraud, lying, or cover-up;
- violations of norms that were readily documentable;
- violations that occurred despite prior negative signals from control bodies; and
- violations that involved important norms of civil or political morality.

Mild censures were levied against

- a body with high prestige;
- a body that had made some effort at reforming the problem at issue; and
- activities that were done on instructions from key political figures.

Under the heading of cases involving fraud, lying, or cover-up, severe censures were leveled against governmental bodies that dealt with building contractors who altered already signed contracts in order to receive higher payments than agreed;[13] and against those that accepted doctored financial reports from institutions receiving governmental aid.[14] Readily documentable faults appeared in the failure of certain local authorities to collect from their residents the minimum levels of taxes and service charges required by the Interior Ministry, and whose collections decreased during the years that were surveyed.[15]

Under the category of actions that proceeded after negative judgments by responsible authorities were excessive payments to certain recipients of National Insurance, which were made despite the finding by the Finance Ministry that they departed from government policy;[16] and the failure of the Defense Ministry to remove a contractor from its list of authorized suppliers despite the contractor's having been found guilty in criminal proceedings, and further having failed to operate according to the ministry's own specifications.[17]

Several items received severe censure for their threat to civil and political norms: excessive and improper detentions of suspects by the police;[18] expenditures of local authorities on public relations that had the effect of subsidizing the reelection campaigns of incumbent officeholders;[19] and benefits paid to elected local officials about to depart from office.[20]

A mild censure was directed against the highly prestigious and prize-winning Society for the Preservation of Nature, despite its having violated rules for the allocation of housing in one of its projects, and for the management of its money and supplies.[21] The Broadcasting Authority received a brief and mild censure despite employing 174 workers in excess of its personnel ceiling, seemingly because it had begun to take corrective steps.[22] The Ministry of Religions also received a mild censure for defects in its financial aid to certain institutions, presumably because it provided the aid on the instructions of political leaders who were members of the government coalition.[23]

Some Difficult Problems on the Boundary between Acceptable Flexibility and Corruption

General guidelines to the differences between acceptable flexibility and corruption in Israeli government do not resolve difficult cases that are near the boundaries of the two concepts. Cases that are especially tricky involve both tacit agreements by policy-making bodies (suggesting acceptable flexibility) and private benefits (suggesting corruption). Two cases in point are the false reports by many civil servants about the kilometers driven on public business, and the commercial banks' manipulation of their shares on the stock exchange.

Is Lying about Kilometrage Corruption When Everyone Does It?

An item in the State Comptroller's *Annual Report* for 1983 described a provision for repaying civil servants who drive their cars on public business.[24] The system allows repayment for up to 500 kilometers per month of within-city driving that are claimed on a general basis, without detailing each trip. According to the report, "Many employees who are owners of automobiles see this as a benefit which they demand in full automatically, without necessary connection with the extent of their actual travels, and *there is a tacit agreement with this notion on the part of officials responsible for the payment of travel expenses*" (italics added).

The State Comptroller showed signs of waffling about this violation. Despite the formal violations and the personal benefits involved, it was not an issue for the Legal Advisor to the Government. It was a poorly disguised fringe benefit that ought to be reformed. The *Report* indicated that the system has negative implication for the tradition of accurate reporting by civil servants, and distorts income opportunities in the favor of employees who own automobiles. While the State Comptroller customarily highlights its conclusions for serious cases in long and detailed summaries, the summary in this case was a mere 7 lines. (An average case involving a violation of the formal rules has a summary of 20 lines, with many of them extending beyond 50 lines.) The recommendation was also modest: "It seems that the responsible persons should arrange a new system that will serve the needs and principles noted."

Profits for Banks and Some Investors at the State's Expense.

While the State Comptroller seemed to signal that false statements by civil servants about their travel is not too bad, he came down hard on the banks' manipulation of their shares.[25] The major banks of the country manipulated their shares for some 11 years before a stock market collapse in October 1983. The banks issued new shares beyond the capacity of the market to absorb them. They urged customers to invest in the shares as a "sure thing," and provided credit for the customers who bought shares. They influenced trust funds under their control to buy their shares, and borrowed heavily to buy shares in their own name. When the public began to lose confidence in the shares, the banks poured up to 44 percent of their total capital into the purchase of their shares in order to maintain their value.

According to the State Comptroller's report, each of these practices violated laws or rules administered by the Bank of Israel, the Securities Commission, the Stock Exchange, or the Finance Ministry. The regulatory bodies overlooked several reports about the banks' practices. Perhaps the banks' practices were acceptable because they succeeded in persuading the public to invest in their shares. This soaked up purchasing power, and provided support to the government's aim (shared by the Finance Ministry and the Bank of Israel) to restrain inflation. Perhaps the Securities Commission and the Stock Exchange were reluctant to impose controls on such major actors in the sale of securities. The banks are the principal stockbrokers in the country. The behavior of the banks became established as precedent. It was awkward for any one of the controllers to step in aggressively while other control bodies acquiesced.

When the market continued to deteriorate beyond the banks' capacity to raise additional capital for propping up their shares, the Finance Ministry agreed to guarantee the value of the shares as per the day prior to the collapse, plus linkage to the value of the U.S. dollar and interest, on condition that the holders of the shares hold them for a fixed period. The State Comptroller estimated that the loss to the State Treasury might reach the equivalent of U.S. $2.5 billion, which is about 10 percent of the current state budget.

The State Comptroller was one of the control agencies that was silent during the many years when the banks manipulated their shares. Once the collapse came, however, the incumbent comptroller reacted with special vigor. The comptroller reads the law to exclude the commercial banks from his orbit; however, he gained access to the scandal via his authority to audit the governmental bodies that control the banks.

The State Comptroller's report about the bank shares stopped short of apportioning blame to the various parties involved, partly because the State Comptroller had no direct access to records of the banks themselves. However, the report left no doubt that some responsibility lay with the banks and with each of several government bodies. The report concluded with a lament about the corruption inherent in mass pursuit after the "golden idol" of easy profit.[26] In keeping with the State Comptroller's recommendation, the Knesset established an extraordinary commission of inquiry to sort out the responsibilities in the crisis.

Corruption and the Limits of Acceptable Flexibility

Why did the State Comptroller react so strongly to the crisis of the bank shares, in contrast with near acquiescence in the false reports by civil servants of their kilometrage? Or in other words, what do the two issues reveal about the kinds of issues that are—and are not—accepted by the informal rules of Israeli government? In both cases there was collusion by responsible authorities. Thus, both seemed to be within the informal rules of the game.

One difference is the sums involved. While false kilometrage added an informal fringe benefit to the salaries of certain civil servants, the costs of the bank scandal may amount to 10 percent of the total government budget.

A second difference is public outcry. As noted in the previous chapter, Israeli incomes typically include a number of fringe benefits that are disguised increments to salary. In these terms the kilometrage of civil servants was their own special deal, not too different from the fringe benefits received by other employees.

The Supreme Court considered the issue of civil servants' kilometrage prior to the State Comptroller. In 1979 a civil servant appealed to the Court, asking that it order the Legal Advisor to the Government and the State Attorney to proceed with criminal charges against another civil servant who lied about his travels. The accused had been ordered to stand before an internal administrative tribunal for a violation of discipline, as opposed to facing a more serious criminal charge.

The judges refused to overturn the decisions of the state's attorneys. They looked on the system of false reports as a serious practice but also noted that it was so widespread as to qualify as an "acceptable lie." Their opinions compared the civil servants' kilometrage to the strange fringe benefits of other employees, and suggested that the system be changed to permit automatic payments for a certain number of kilometers each month, without requiring false reports.[27]

In contrast to the near-conventional issue of the civil servants' fringe benefits, the crisis of the banks shares threatened a form of savings widely used by Israelis. It dominated the news until the Finance Ministry decided to protect investors against loss. Later there was extensive media coverage of the State Comptroller's *Report* on the issue, and the commission of inquiry.

Conclusions

Clear instances of governmental corruption in Israel resemble those in other Western democracies. Fraudulant distortions of public allocations for private benefit are likely to result in criminal prosecutions. However, Israel is marked more than other Western democracies by a large public sector, and an extensive network of formal control mechanisms. Its officials have evolved informal rules that are more permissive than the formal rules. Surpassing the formal rules is widely acknowledged, and justified as the only way to govern a country that has enacted too many restrictions. It is easier to accept departures from the formal rules than to eliminate the surplus rules.

The informal rules permit flexibility within the framework of centralized controls. They allow discretion at working levels, which extends to formal violations of the laws. Sometimes this discretion is asserted by entrepreneurial heads of local authorities or other governmental bodies who act without prior approvals. At other times it is arrived at via bargaining with the officials responsible for the implementation of formal controls.

While informality allows flexibility, it also causes confusion. Officials, contractors, and average citizens have difficulty knowing what is permissible, and what is corruption. Although the formal norms are published and clear, the informal norms have blurred boundaries that may not be recognized until they are surpassed. When control bodies wish, they can bring the full weight of their formal sanctions against hapless individuals who might have thought themselves within the boundaries of the informal norms.

The informal limits of flexibility take account of the resources at stake; the willingness of other officials to accept the departure from formal norms; the concern shown for the issue by the mass media; indications of fraud, lying or cover-up for personal profit; the ease of documenting the departures from formal norms; and the risk from the behavior to important civil and political norms. These vague limits do not allow the unambiguous definition of what is permitted, and what is not. They must be used with a sense of judgment as to what is accceptable, and with some good luck that an official will not be inclined to an unusually strict interpretation of the formal rules.

Notes

1. See Nathanial H. Leff, "Economic Development through Bureaucratic Corruption," in *Political Corruption: Readings in Comparative Analysis* ed. Arnold J. Heidenheimer (New York: Holt, Rinehart & Winston, 1970), pp 510-20.
2. James C. Scott, *Comparative Political Corruption* (Englewood Cliffs, N.J.: Prentice-Hall, 1972), p. x.
3. *Report on the Bank Shares—the Crisis of October, 1983* (Jerusalem: State Comptroller, 1984) (Hebrew).
4. Here the discussion focuses on governmental corruption, and not what may be termed a larger conception of societal corruption, as discussed in J. Patrick Dobel, "The Corruption of a State," *American Political Science Review* 72 (September 1978): 958-73.
5. Joseph J. Senturia, "Corruption, Political," in *Encyclopedia of the Social Sciences*, vol. 4 (New York: Crowell-Collier-Macmillan, 1930-35), p. 449, as cited in Heidenheimer, *Political Corruption*, "Introduction".
6. J. S. Nye, "Corruption and Political Development: A Cost-Benefit Analysis," and Arnold A. Rogow and H. D. Lasswell, "The Definition of Corruption," both in *Political Corruption: Readings in Comparative Analysis*, ed. Arnold J.

Heidenheimer (New York: Holt, Rinehart & Winston, 1970) pp. 564-78 and 54-55.

7. John G. Peters and Susan Welch, "Political Corruption in America: A Search for Definitions and a Theory," *American Political Science Review* 72 (September 1978): 974-84.

8. For an example of the work done by the State Comptroller's staff, outside their formal responsibilities, see B. Geist, ed., *State Audit: Developments in Public Accountability* (London: Macmillan, 1981).

9. State Comptroller Law, 5718-1958, Sections. 9 and 10.

10. 1977 version, Section 286.

11. Shmuel Holander, "Suspicion of Criminal Activity: Section 14c of the State Comptroller Law," *Iyunim* (Journal of the State Comptroller's staff) 24 (1975): 17-21 (Hebrew).

12. Bernard Berelson, *Content Analysis in Communications Research* (New York: Free Press, 1952).

13. *Annual Report #35*, pp. 177-88.

14. *Ibid.*, pp. 320-25.

15. *Ibid.*, pp. 916-31.

16. *Ibid.*, pp. 803-08.

17. *Ibid.*, pp. 1008-13.

18. *Ibid.*, pp. 435-58.

19. *Ibid.*, pp. 880-90.

20. *Ibid.*, pp. 890-902.

21. *Annual Report #34*, pp. 279-85.

22. *Ibid.*, pp. 646-51.

23. *Ibid.*, pp. 224-36.

24. Pp. 1-7 (Hebrew).

25. See the *Report* cited above.

26. *Report*, p. 102.

27. Suit of Shmuel Vinograd against Legal Advisor to the Government; State Attorney; and Yaacov Malkai, National Traffic Supervisor. #665/79. *Judgments*, vol. 34, pt. 2, 1980 (Hebrew).

12

Perspective on Israel's Political Economy

Israel is a fascinating site for research about political economy. The interpenetration of its politics and its economics is profound. There is no other Western democracy where the public sector accounts for such a proportion of the economy's wherewithal. During 1985 there was no other issue that has commanded as much attention in Israel as the government's policies for economic stability. With all the importance accorded to economic issues, they appear in a context where other issues are important as well. For most of Israel's history, issues of defense, housing, economic development, education, and other kinds of service provision have been more important than economic tidiness with low inflation.

Israel's society and politics is a rich stew of contending interests and perspectives. Furthermore, the cooking is done under the pressure of personal and community anxiety. Although this book has focused on several issues in the arena of politics and national economic policy, it should not conclude without describing other perspectives and issues.

The Pressures of Israel Written Small

For most people, the environment they see is not the macro world of national statistics. For the typical Israeli in 1985, the economic side of personal life was pressing. Salaries were eroding in real terms, as cost-of-living adjustments were kept below the rate of inflation. Income erosion had become an element in the policy to reduce purchasing power, as a way of coping with inflation. The take-home pay of senior professors had fallen to less than the equivalent of U.S. $700 per month, and that of specialist physicians attached to major hospitals to about $600. Both of these groups, like most other occupations in Israel are paid according to national scales, and both are considered to be well paid. Further down the scale were the employees of many small industries, whose monthly income was likely to be in the range of $300. After yet another deliberate erosion in salaries that began in early July, the finance minister revealed that his monthly take-home pay amounted to only $591.[1]

Low income was not the only sign of economic distress that was apparent to the individual Israeli. The employees of numerous factories recognized the difficulties faced by their employers: a falloff in overseas orders due to the overvalued Israeli shekel, and a reluctance to continue production for the Israeli market, where a squeeze between controlled prices and increasing costs made the enterprise less profitable. For some cases, the additional problems of old equipment and lackluster management had brought the factories to a condition of bankruptcy and dependence on periodic infusions of government aid.

In public-service sectors, economic pressures prevented the recruitment of new personnel to keep up with client demands, or forced cutbacks from existing staff. University professors found themselves teaching larger classes, and doing more of the clerical work. Personnel in hospitals found themselves facing longer lines of patients, and felt less able than usual to attend properly to the needs of each. Even the simple task of paying one's monthly bills was made onerous by the long queues that formed at the beginning and middle of each month at the post office. (The postal branches accepted payments for utility bills without imposing a service charge, while the commercial banks charged for the service.) Because of the crowds who were paying their bills, Israelis also found it difficult to buy stamps or mail packages at the beginning or the middle of the month.

Other pressures were even more severe than the economic. The physician, professor, and factory worker were likely to meet and gripe about their problems while serving in the military. Through the early months of 1985 their meeting might have occurred in a Lebanese combat zone. If not, the thought of such an experience could not be far from their minds. A typical male between the ages of 22 and 55 spent upward of 60 days in the active reserves during 1984-85. Early in 1985 there was a wave of suicide attacks on Israeli units carried out by young Shiite Moslems. Most of the killed and injured Israelis were young men in their late teens and twenties, but some were reservists in their late thirties and forties. The news of such deaths was made no less threatening by the realization that the Israeli army was well on its way out of Lebanon, and each death might be the last.

Economically Induced Travel Restrictions: Prisoners of Zion?

Many Israelis seek escape from the rigors of their national existence via foreign travel. Most countries of their region are closed to them, and so a trip to Europe is a popular way of breaking loose. During 1982 the number of departures by residents equaled 16 percent of the population.[2]

The very act of leaving Israel on a holiday had become an exercise even more complex than usual. Thorough security checks at the airport have long been a feature of Israeli life, meant to insure the passengers' safety.

Other checks are designed to insure that the travel does not endanger the state by draining the economy, or taking too many of its potential soldiers out of the country at any one time. The economic controls increased dramatically in the spring and summer of 1985.

- The typical adult male requires a document from his military unit authorizing his departure from the country.
- Travel taxes accumulated in stages in response to the decline in the country's foreign currency reserves; in July 1983 they amounted to a $300 levy on each resident leaving the country, plus 20 percent of the value of the airline ticket, 15 percent of any other travel services purchased from Israel (hotels, car rentals), 15 percent on the foreign currency that was purchased for use abroad, as well as the $10 airport tax paid on actual departure.
- Along with the increase in travel taxes there was a decrease in the amount of foreign currency that a resident was allowed to purchase and take out of the country; the amount allowed per resident in July 1985 was $800.
- Extracting the $800 from one's bank was an exercise in itself. It was necessary to present an airline ticket, passport, and the receipt for the $300 travel tax; each of these was stamped by the bank when the foreign currency or traveler's checks were handed over, and the amount of the funds received was indicated alongside each stamp.

It was for all these reasons that Israelis opposed to travel restrictions—led by travel agents who saw themselves losing business by the controls—dubbed themselves the prisoners of Zion. The reference was to the Russian Jews who could not emigrate to the Promised Land and had labeled themselves the prisoners of Zion.

Security as Ubiquitous Issue

No consideration of Israeli public policy can stray far from the issue of security. The society does not seem as vulnerable as it did in 1948 or 1967, when Arab armies from several countries massed on the borders and Arab leaders threatened annihilation. To date, however, only Egypt from among the Arab countries has agreed to a formal peace with Israel, and that peace is not fulfilled as promised. Hardly any Egyptian tourists come to Israel, there are few business contacts between the two countries, and the Egyptian media periodically engage in vitriolic anti-Semitism. Some other Arab countries engage in under-the-table dealings with Israel, yet their formal policies and sometimes the statements of their leaders recall the nightmares of 1948. For the Israeli population that includes many survivors of the

European Holocaust and persecutions in Arab lands, Arab rhetoric recalls the too-recent past, and shapes political attitudes that are wary of compromise on issues of security.

Critics of Israeli policy and culture—from within and outside the country—cite the country for an obsession with the dark side of Jewish history. Former Prime Minister Menachem Begin personified this obsession, which came to light in his discussions with (some would say his lectures to) foreign officials and journalists. Begin and many other Israelis explain their preoccupation with history as legitimate, which Jews and Gentiles must accept as an explanation and justification for Israel's concern with its contemporary security.

Whether obsession, preoccupation, or legitimate concern, horrid memories reappear each spring, when a day to remember the victims of the Holocaust precedes by one week a day to remember the people who fell in the defense of Israel. National television features graphic films and personal reports by survivors of the Holocaust prior to each Holocaust Remembrance Day, and interviews with the wives, children, and parents of fallen soldiers prior to each Memorial Day. In 1985 the two-week agony was prolonged and deepened. It was the fortieth anniversary of the Nazis' defeat; there was prolog and epilog to President Ronald Reagan's visit to the German war cemetery at Bitburg, which included the graves of Nazi Waffen SS troops as well as the graves of common German soldiers; and a renewed search for Nazi war criminal Dr. Josef Menegele, widely known for his cruel experiments on concentration camp inmates.

Political Parties

Parties are the stuff of Israeli politics, yet none has ever been able to overcome all the opposition and win a majority in a national election. Because the Knesset is built upon strict proportional representation, no party has ever been able to rule without the fetters of coalition partners.[3]

After the 1984 election produced a fine division between the two major groupings (Labour Alignment and Likud), they agreed to an unusual National Unity Government. According to the formal agreement, Labour's Shimon Peres will serve as prime minister for two years, and then switch places with the foreign minister, Likud's Yitzhak Shamir. The present government is also unusual in that no religious party can grant or deny crucial votes to the coalition leaders. Each of the religious parties that had been prominent in the past is suffering from internal splits; however, neither of the major secular parties seems willing to offend the basic postures of religious parties. The religious parties may be important again.

Coalition governments are thought to be timid. Heroic behavior by the leader of any one party is constrained by the lack of a majority in the Knesset and the prospect of a government collapse, yet Israeli governments have been stable. The average time between elections has been more than three years (the legal limit is four years). Perhaps the perennial failure of any party to win a majority encourages stability. No party that causes a crisis is likely to end up in control of a united government.

The present government has been on the verge of one crisis or another ever since its creation. Conflicts among the coalition partners have focused on key political appointments, the postures to be taken with respect to discussions with Egypt, Jordan, and Palestinians, and economic issues.

One party conflict that is close to the surface concerns the war in Lebanon. Members of the Labour Alignment have called for an inquiry into the origins and conduct of the war. According to many anticipations, such an inquiry would not cast favorable light on the record of Ariel Sharon, who was defense minister during much of the war and is currently the minister of trade and industry. Members of the Likud Bloc, which dominated the government during most of the war, have opposed such an inquiry to the extent of threatening to depart the government (and thereby cause its collapse) if an inquiry goes forward.

A phenomenon that combines party with economic considerations was the experience of Yitzhak Modei, who served as finance minister from the beginning of the Government of National Unity in 1984 to April 1986. Modei is a member of the Liberal party within the Likud bloc. He had to cope with opposition to his policies that comes from other wings of Likud—including from within the contentious Liberal party itself—as well as from the Labour party. Some of his proposals for cutting the budget ran aground on the opposition of populist Likud members like housing minister David Levy and labour and welfare minister Moshe Katzav. One proposal to impose a small fee for each visit with a physician ran afoul of the Labour party health minister, Mordecai Gur. Yet other proposals of the finance minister encountered the opposition of Labour party member Gad Yabobi, who is minister of the economy. The Ministry of the Economy is a pale shadow of the Finance Ministry in terms of its functions and professional personnel. It was created during the Begin government to provide yet another portfolio for distribution to its political supporters. Nonetheless, it gives to its minister a certain prominence in the field of economic policy, and provides a stage for alternative policy proposals. Modei presided over a dramatic decline in Israel's inflation rate, detailed in chapter 7. However, he was forced out as finance minister when he expressed in public sharp criticism of prime minister Shimon Peres (Labour party) when Peres supported special government funding for a hard pressed building company owned by the Labour Federation (also controlled by the Labour party).

Again, The Prominant Features of Israel's Political Economy

The governments that are headed by finely-balanced political coalitions control the overwhelming proportion of Israel's economy. The government sector is so dominant that indicators that are useful in most other Western democracies—like GNP and personal income—are misleading in Israel's case.

The pressures on Israeli policymakers are weightier than in other Western countries. There is a shortage of resources, service demands are intense, and a large share of resources is preempted by defense. Israeli politics rewards entrepreneurial behavior. The complexity of issues demands indirection in policy-making. The multiplicity of governmental controls requires that many are overlooked in the interest of manageability. Knowing the informal limits of power is one mark of the sophisticated Israeli policymaker.

Entrepreneurialism, indirection, and flexibility help to make things a bit more tolerable. They also cause problems. Throughout the 1977-84 period, entrepreneurialism and indirection favored those who requested resources more than those who would limit the allocation of resources. As a result, these behaviors contributed to excessive government outlays. A tolerance for those who break the formal rules for the good of the public may encourage some public officials to break the rules for their personal benefit. Along with entrepreneurialism and indirection, flexibility with respect to the formal rules makes for a lack of tidiness, predictability, and discipline in Israeli public life.

Israelis have not learned the conventional lessons of how to live within their means. For many of them, economizing has been less important than accomplishing substantive goals.

Notes

1. *Ma'Ariv*, July 9, 1985 (Hebrew).
2. Some of these departures were individuals who traveled more than once during the year. *Statistical Abstract of Israel, 1983* (Jerusalem: Central Bureau of Statistics, 1984), p. 123.
3. For a general overview of Israeli politics see Asher Arian, *Politics in Israel: The Second Generation* (Chatham, N.J.: Chatham House, 1985).

Epilog
For Those Who Think That Political
Scientists Should Advise Politicians

At the end of a book that deals with Israel's economic problems and the behavior of its policymakers, a reader might feel entitled to a prescription: What should policymakers do in order to cure their country's problems? Those expecting a clear answer to this question are not familiar with my previous work, or my approach to political analysis. My commitment is to the description of important events and analysis directed at explanation. Several years of inquiry into Israel's political economy have strengthened me in this approach. The details encountered by Israeli politicians move faster than I can think or write. The most that I can offer is general observation and guidance.

What I have described in this book is a complex set of economic and political conditions, which operated to produce an unconventional and troubling picture. Israel's government dominates the nation's economy to an extent that is comparable with the Eastern Bloc. High inflation was chronic for several years, and may return again. There is also an imbalance in foreign trade, a substantial foreign debt, and foreign currency reserves that have depended on extraordinary aid from the United States government. Unemployment is higher than normal. Immigration has all but stopped, except for a wave of Ethiopians and a dribble of Westerners. There are problems in measuring emigration; however, those who worry about the issue see a significant increase over the recent past.

Proposals for Economic Reform

There is no end of proposals for the repair of Israel's economy. University economists advise the government, write for the popular press, and find defects in each government policy—sometimes minutes after the latest policy has been made public. The problem is not a failure of economic wisdom or a lack of options. The basic problem during much of 1977-85 may have been the style of Israeli politics. Economists, other option makers, and critics seemed more nearly part of the problem than likely

149

sources of solution. What was missing was political discipline, a restraint on criticism, and a capacity of the government to stick to any one of several reasonable programs. A lack of restraint and inhibition in Israel's democracy seemed to work against its economic problems.

This should not be read as a diatribe against democracy. It should be read as a suggestion in behalf of restraint in public life. As a result of my efforts to describe the gaming that occurs among policy actors (in various chapters called entrepreneurialism, indirection, and flexibility with respect to the application of formal rules), I am convinced that this gaming has made policy-making more exciting but not better. A lack of discipline in the economy was one of the factors associated with high inflation. Persistent gaming among policymakers and a lack of regard for the formal rules have contributed to inflation and the other economic problems associated with it.

What is to be done? I join with the general sentiment that advocates significant cuts in the programs of government and other public-sector bodies. I will avoid identifying what is superfluous, and what essential on the menu of public services. This argument has been endless, and more troubling than enlightening. I am less inclined to offer detailed solutions than to make the most general kinds of observations. In any case, the policymakers in charge have to decide, with an eye to the current realities in the usually intense competition among parties, factions, and individuals. My general points are the following:

1. Do something. Formulate a reasonable set of proposals that have a chance of surviving the gaming that will take place among supporters and antagonists, then stick to it. Grand pronouncements that are soon diluted or forgotten altogether leave the public confused and cynical. An intelligent and tolerant public is one of democracy's most valued assets. Among the tensions felt by Israelis are those that come from the posturing of policymakers who can make declarations but who cannot implement.

2. Determine priorities. Policymakers must recognize the variety of interests and perspectives in their polity but know that they cannot please everyone. If it is important to tidy up the economy, then some interests are going to suffer more than others, at least in the short term. If it is not possible to make some suffer in the short run, then all may suffer greatly in the long term. Democracy offers a way of choosing those who will suffer most: duly elected members of the government can argue and then vote about their priorities. "Politics" should not be a forbidden principle; it is crucial to the operation of democracy. Primarily it is necessary to decide. The endless handwringing of politicians too soft to make tough decisions risks the loss of support in the public at large.

3. When a policy is adopted, stick to it. Persistent criticism is debilitating. Israeli democracy is served well enough by intragovernmental debate before a policy is adopted. It is threatened by a surplus of intragovernmental dispute after a policy is adopted. Criticism must be tolerated from the parliamentary opposition but not from members of the government. The ancient Greeks knew the difference between democracy and anarchy. Modern Israelis who do not recognize that difference risk their democracy.

Israeli policymakers have proven themselves more capable in issues of defense than in issues of economic policy. They have initiated combat in order to serve vital interests, and then joined bereaved families in mourning the losses. Threats of economic disorder did not provoked the same kind of heroic decision making. The government dithered less over issues of life and death than over the issue of aiding an uncompetitive clothing firm where the risk is one of a few hundred jobs. This is understandable, insofar as the immediate consequences of economic inaction are less threatening than the immediate consequences of military inaction. In the longer run, however, the lack of decisiveness in the economic realm threatens the weakness and the independence of the nation.

Perhaps the Answer Is Electoral Reform?

Some Israelis think that the economic problems of their society result from the way the citizens choose their representatives in the Knesset. Proportional representation has been effective in translating into the Knesset the political divisions that exist in the electorate. Every government has been a coalition of several parties, each of which must accept some demands from its partners.

Perhaps a change in the electoral system will help one or another party attain a majority in a national election, and thereby produce a government that is more united and more capable of making difficult economic decisions. Without a need to pay off numerous coalition partners, the government can decide which programs should be sacrificed and begin an era when government outlays are more in keeping with its resources.

One proposal is to retain proportional representation but to increase the minimum percentage of votes that a party must win inorder to receive seats in the Knesset. Upping the percentage from 1 to 5, for example, would eliminate a number of small parties and leave more seats for the major parties to divide among themselves.

Another proposal is to create legislative districts, in place of the single national polling that is used now for choosing members of the Knesset.

With a bit of gerrymandering, the electoral districts could produce a Knesset majority for a party even if there was no majority for it in the country.

Against these proposals are several inhibitions that so far have kept Israeli politicians from changing the character of national elections.

- Electoral reform would not rid the society of the underlying differences that give rise to the country's political parties. Israel is a diverse society, even within its Jewish majority. There are different life-styles and some suspicions among Jews whose families, until recently, spent centuries soaking up cultures as diverse as those of North and South America, Eastern and Western Europe, North Africa, Central Asia, India, Yemen, and Ethiopia. Ideology is another source of division. Doctrines of the Labour Alignment put the emphasis on social and economic equality, while those of the Likud Bloc feature nationalism (the focus of its Herut faction) or free enterprise (the focus of its Liberal faction), with a substantial dose of populism. The deepest conflicts among the Jews may be those that set the secular majority against those who define themselves as religious.
- The present institutional arrangements—with all their problems—may at least keep the country's social tensions from boiling over into physical conflict. A reform of the electoral system may lessen the power of minor parties but also create bitter frustrations among those who lose power. Israeli politicians are sensitive to historical splits that exposed Jews to defeat and destruction at the hands of foreign enemies.
- Some opposition to electoral reform comes from the simple fear of incumbents that a change will endanger their personal and party fortunes. Bold politicians will occasionally reform the structure that has nurtured them. Yet most politicians seem more willing to put up with the problems of the present than to risk outcomes that may be worse.

In fact, the problem of Israeli governments that have trouble making unpleasant economic decisions is not clearly one of the interparty conflict! Throughout the period of the Likud bloc's 1977-84 domination of the government, which was marked by an increase in the annual rate of inflation from 35 to 400 percent, the several finance ministers who sought to cut the government's outlays had as much trouble with ministers of their own party as with ministers of their coalition partners.[1] This suggests that a deeply rooted competitiveness and seeking after advantage is more important than electoral machines in creating the lack of economic discipline in Israeli governments.

Israel's high inflation declined dramatically during 1985-86. Part of the explanation was a greater than normal willingness of leading politicians to deny economic benefits to claimants among their supporters. However, these same politicians have so far lacked the will or the discipline to implement all of the economic reforms that they have proclaimed. Inflation may move upward again under the pressure of deferred demands. No certain fix for Israel's political economy appears on the horizon. Policymakers must cope with irresistible demands on limited national resources, and with the problematic features of their own political style.

Note

1. See my *What Makes Israel Tick? or How Domestic Policymakers Cope with Constraints* (Chicago: Nelson-Hall, 1985), esp. ch. 3.

Index

155